EARS & BUBBLES

Ears & Bubbles

DANCING MY WAY FROM THE MICKEY MOUSE CLUB TO THE LAWRENCE WELK SHOW

Bobby Burgess

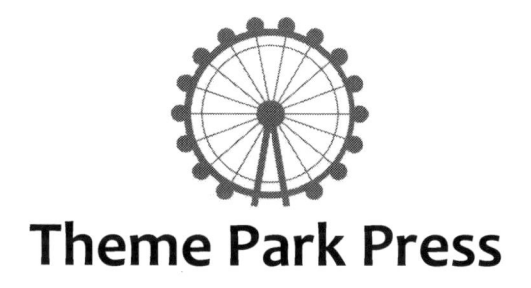

Theme Park Press

© **2014 BOBBY BURGESS**

All rights reserved. No part of this book may be reproduced in any written or electronic medium without written permission of the publisher, except in the case of brief quotations or excerpts embodied in critical articles or reviews provided to the general public free of charge and for non-commercial purposes.

Although every precaution has been taken to verify the accuracy of the information contained herein, no responsibility is assumed for any errors or omissions, and no liability is assumed for damages that may result from the use of this information.

The views expressed in this book are those of the author alone.

This book is an independent publication. Any references to copyrighted or trademarked intellectual property are made strictly for editorial purposes, and no commercial claim upon that property is made by Theme Park Press or the author.

Theme Park Press publishes its books in a variety of print and electronic formats. Some content that appears in one format may not appear in another.

Editor: Bob McLain
Layout: Artisanal Text
Cover Design: Emily White

ISBN 978-1-941500-07-1
10 9 8 7 6 5 4 3 2 1
Printed in the United States of America

Theme Park Press | www.ThemeParkPress.com
Address queries to bob@themeparkpress.com

This book is dedicated to my three families: my loving, close personal one, my Mouseketeer family, and my Lawrence Welk musical family for all the enjoyment they've all given me throughout my life.

Contents

Introduction   ix

Born to Dance   1

What's a Mouseketeer?   9

We're a Hit!   21

Where Do I Go from Here?   29

The Next Big Break   43

The Welk Family   49

Changing Partners   57

Lawrence Welk   65

Welkisms   77

On the Road   91

All Over the Map   97

Cotillion Master   105

Around the World   109

The Best of Times   115

All in a Day's Work   121

Lucky Me   133

Farewells   139

Acknowledgments   141

About the Author   143

About the Publisher   145

More Books from Theme Park Press   147

Introduction

Lawrence Welk once said, "I never had any trouble with Bobby because he was raised by Walt Disney." What a wonderful quote, and one that I will never forget. I was one lucky guy going from one family institution to another.

Imagine appearing on the three original seasons of *The Mickey Mouse Club* (1955-1959) and then having several generations of kids worldwide enjoy the show through reruns that lasted over thirty years. Even today the original *Mickey Mouse Club* is available on DVD and my own grandkids get to see me singing and dancing as a child.

What wonderful memories I have to share with you about those early years with my fellow Mouseketeers—and beyond, because we're still doing Disney shows, conventions, and appearances to this day. In fact, many of the Mouseketeers are like a second family to me, and we still see each other often. And with the 60th anniversary of *The Mickey Mouse Club* coming in 2015, I'd call that an incredibly successful run of both the show and the friendships that have lasted through the decades.

Being one of the lucky "roll-call" Mouseketeers who appeared in every episode of the original series, that time brings back lots of great memories of my fellow Mice and the fun, hard work and incredible journey we shared. We spent a lot of time together, because not only did we film at the Disney Studio, but we often appeared at Disneyland and even went on the road to meet and greet the thousands of young fans who tuned in to *The Mickey Mouse Club* every day.

When we were kids we really didn't appreciate what was going on around us…the success of the show, the ability to ride the attractions at Disneyland to our hearts content, and the privilege it was to work with Walt Disney himself. But today, all of us realize what a profound time it was. In the mid 1950's the Disney Studio was in full swing with animated classics in the making such as *Sleeping Beauty* and *Lady and the Tramp*, television production being stepped up with our show and the weekly *Disneyland* series, and Walt Disney walking the Studio grounds every day getting ready to open the world's first theme park, Disneyland. Even with all the goings-on, Mr. Disney managed to keep a close eye on us kids on the set, albeit somewhat covertly from behind the scenes. More about that later.

And then, just three years after *The Mickey Mouse Club* ended, I became a regular dancing cast member on *The Lawrence Welk Show*, a series that ultimately proved to be one of television's longest running and best loved musical variety hours, still in reruns today. I had twenty-one years of dancing up a storm with three different dancing partners on the show. And not only did I get to dance and sing with all the other cast members every week but we often traveled around the country through those years, and still do today, appearing at fairs, festivals, and theaters-in-the-round, and we even entertained regularly in Branson, Missouri, the Midwest capital of song and dance.

Twenty-one years is a long time on one show and I had so many adventures and great stories from that time that I will share with you in this book, including finding the girl of my dreams, getting married, raising four wonderful children, and now having grandkids (even though I'm still a kid at heart myself!).

While I wear my "entertainer" hat all the time, I also wear others: husband, father, grandfather, world traveler, and business owner (having established the "Burgess Cotillion" to teach children ballroom dancing and proper manners). You'll read about all those roles in this book.

As I said, I'm a lucky guy. I hope you enjoy my memories of a great time singing and dancing my way through the years. I can't imagine a happier life.

Bobby Burgess
June 2014

CHAPTER ONE

Born to Dance

As soon as I could walk, I was turning and twirling to the music on the radio. When I was about four years old, Mom gave me tap dancing lessons. When I would learn a new step, I would immediately put on my tap shoes and say to whoever would listen, "Do you want to see my new dance?"

I was born in Long Beach, California, on May 19, 1941, the second of four children to Janie Mae Burgess, my mom and a stay-at-home housewife, and Bill Burgess, known as Eddie, my dad and a 9-5 meat cutter, or butcher, at Safeway.

Mom was a friendly, outgoing lady who everyone loved. She was that typical 1950s stay-at-home mother whose family was number one with her. She didn't believe in babysitters, so she took us everyplace! She also took me faithfully to all my lessons, sometimes driving for hours for tap, jazz, accordion, and more. But she was not a pushy showbiz mom, just a devoted one. She was a California native, born in 1912, and she graduated from Long Beach Poly High School in 1936, as did my siblings and I in later years.

Her favorite place was the beach, and as a girl she enjoyed swimming around Rainbow Pier in Long Beach. Tennis was another of her passions, and even in her later years, she would rise at 4am to watch a live tennis match. She actually became a minister in the Four Square Church mentored by Evangelist Aimee Semple McPherson at Angeles Temple. She even dated Aimee's son, and then went on to play piano and preach for the church in Colorado and elsewhere.

And fishing—she would sit for hours at lakes, streams, and ocean piers. Slot machines were another passion in Vegas and at Indian casinos. She was a sun-worshipper, too; on went the baby oil and out on the float went mom.

She had the same hairdo her whole adult life and slept in soft curlers every night as soon as those were invented. Her hair was poufy in front and on the top of her head, and then feathered around her face and falling into shoulder-length curls around the bottom, the popular look of the 1940s. Most of the time, she was a dyed redhead.

Dad was a dapper guy. He never wore jeans. Even when he took us horseback riding, camping, or fishing, it was always in slacks, belt, sport coat, and hard-soled shoes. He wore his hair slicked back with pomade. You always knew if Dad was teasing you because he would bite his tongue and stick it out the side of his mouth with a devilish look in his eye. Dad, again, was that 1950s dad, a 9-to-5 worker, 6 days a week, a provider. He loved his baseball teams and shared that love with us, his family. He craved peanuts and ice cream. He delivered meat in Canada, came out to California in 1928, met my mom through mutual friends, and they stayed married for 59 years, a happy union. Many years later, it was my pleasure to give them a vacation trip to Hawaii, my mom's favorite destination, for seventeen years in a row.

My older brother, Bill, had an aptitude for fixing cars. His Dodge Charger went for 360,000 miles. Bill was a very successful grocery store manager. But when I later gave him dance lessons, uh oh, he had two left feet! We all have our own special talents. I was a fun Uncle Bob to Bill's four kids, Cheri, Teri, Ricky, and Michele, which was good practice for when I became a dad myself many years later. My sisters are Bette and Barbara. Bette loved sports and riding horses, and Barb was into hairdressing, animals, and nature.

At home, we had a menagerie of dogs, cats, and birds. Mom raised canaries and sold them to the local pet shop. One day someone left the cage door open and they all flew away. The trees and phone wires were full of canaries in differing shades of yellow. Dad would take the bus to work and on returning every night, our two cats, Mr. Man and Mousey, would meet him at the corner and accompany him home. One of my favorite dogs was a Hungarian Puli given to me by Moochie, aka Kevin Corcoran of *The Mickey Mouse Club*, whose family raised them. We had desert tortoises too.

Myrtle the Turtle was a particular favorite whose back scales we colored in different rainbow shades. Our dogs all had "B" names just like my brothers and sisters had "B" names -- Bill, Bobby, Bette, and Barbara. Se we had Buttons, Betsy, B.O., and Babe. We had fish tanks bubbling throughout the house. My grandma and grandpa, Baba and Dada, had ducks called Sadie and Leon which were my grandparents' actual names. One night when we were sitting down to a delicious duck dinner, we noticed Sadie and Leon were missing. Uh oh!

In the 1950s living in Long Beach was not like today with high rises, corporations, and banks. Then it was a huge navy town, with an important navy base to the west. Being from Signal Hill, an incorporated tiny town within Long Beach, our town's income was from oil. Everywhere you'd look, there were oil derricks—steel and wooden like a forest. On occasion the wooden derricks would catch fire, at which time big brother Bill would hustle me and my sisters into his jalopy to go watch the spectacle. I even made some money making lemonade and Kool-Aid with my little neighbor girlfriend and selling it to the oil workers—water, powder, sugar, and mix. All packed into my little red wagon.

Downtown Pine Avenue was our retail destination. There were no shopping malls. During World War II, as a little boy, I remember air raid practice. We'd have to blackout the house and position ourselves under mattresses and tables. Living near the airport and Douglas Aircraft, authorities would place camouflage nets over Douglas to disguise it like a field so enemy aircraft wouldn't recognize the factory.

Signal Hill was a friendly town and we kids would play kick-the-can in the street or hide-and-seek all over the neighborhood. Everyone would go all out for the carnival at school. I especially loved the Halloween carnivals. I won several costume contests. Once I dressed as Mortimer Snerd (a well-known ventriloquist's dummy). Another time I got a friend to help me be a four-legged, two-man horse. In later years on *The Lawrence Welk Show*, with Jack Imel my fellow tap dancer, we would be assigned to dance as a horse, a cow, or a bull. We'd flip a coin to see who would be the rear end. Whoever lost got the dubious honors.

Doors weren't locked in those days, and us kids were always running around making forts or exploring caves just at the end of the street in the oil fields where the 405 Freeway now roars by. Like a lot of boys in the 50s, I had a paper route. One year, I was so successful with "starts" (new subscribers) that I won a fun trip to P.O.P—Pacific Ocean Park, a popular amusement park on Santa Monica Beach. I had a happy childhood and enjoyed so many family outings.

Mom and Dad would take us to the beach, the favorite swimming holes in the San Gabriel Mountains, and the drive-in. Dad would also take us to the jalopy races and occasionally the horse races. He loved his racing form and betting on the ponies.

Sundays, more often than not, Mom would make a delicious roast for dinner. She was a great cook. Dad would take me to the Strand

Theater on the Pike (dining and entertainment location in Long Beach) to see gangster or western movies, and vaudeville acts. The Pike was the greatest amusement park with the greatest roller coaster, of which I'm an aficionado, called the Cyclone or Jack Rabbit Racer, with the world's steepest drop. Many drunken sailors were killed because they would stand up right before the big dip and fall to their deaths. At the foot of the roller coaster was the free Punch and Judy puppet show that was always hilarious to me. What a great childhood!

In the 1950s, amateur television shows were the thing. I loved them, and my dance teacher matched me up with my first dance partner, Judy Lewis. Judy and I were teamed up at Richards and Martins dance school in Anaheim. She was a cute, blonde tapper with a big smile.

We were "Bobby and Judy". We got together at age five and broke up at eight. But it did give me my first taste of dancing as part of a team, a hint of my future many years down the road. Judy and I tapped, did Hawaiian dances, cakewalks, and appeared at fairs and service clubs, mostly free for the experience, but occasionally for five or ten dollars.

My favorite memory of us was at age six. We appeared at the huge Shrine Auditorium in Los Angeles, and we followed the Will Mastin Trio featuring Sammy Davis, Jr. tap dancing and playing the drums. He was sensational even then as a teenager. I was mesmerized watching from the wings. Now it was our turn. The lights were bright, and we became disoriented. So we ended up dancing our "I Got Rhythm" tap dance facing the curtains! But we still got a nice hand, along with a few laughs, as we finally turned around, bowed, and ran off.

One memory was an unusual one. Judy and I would occasionally appear in a minstrel show. It seems like it was for the Shriners, but I just remember sitting on stage next to all these men in blackface, and we'd do our routines when called on. We were probably seven or eight years old.

As a solo tap dancer, my specialty was dancing really fast. "Twelfth Street Rag" and "Limehouse Blues" were two of my best routines. The amateur shows were Hollywood based, and even though they didn't pay money, they gave you loot if you won. I did 75 of these shows and ended up winning a bike, a watch, a washing machine, and even a fish aquarium that is one of my hobbies to this day. These shows had names like *Hollywood Opportunity*, *Backstage with N.T.G.*, and *Your*

Town's Talent. On the latter, I tapped to "You Are My Lucky Star" and was called over to be interviewed. The emcee said, "I understand you have a birthmark in the shape of a star. Where is it?" My reply: "I'm sitting on it!" That's right, folks, on my left buttock I have a perfect 5-point, pink star birthmark. And I won that contest.

I also won a week's appearance on the Al Jarvis television show and did a different dance every day. The show was a local TV talent series. If you won, the prize was a paid engagement. Al was a big, friendly entrepreneur who liked to give talented young stars a break. He started in radio, but it was his successful television show that made him famous.

His girl Friday was Betty White. She was just so friendly. When I told her I was from Long Beach, she said her fan club president lived there. We later came to find out that her fan club leader was our neighbor!

Getting me to my dancing adventures was usually left to my mom who drove me just about everywhere, although I loved Dad to take me to gigs because he would buy me a banana split afterward for a job well done. On one of these amateur shows, a Hollywood agent was watching. She called the station and said, "I think I can give this boy some work." This was famous child agent Hazel McMillan. Now, let me tell you a little secret. My mom would grease the wheels with Hazel by always sending her a little thank-you note with Hazel's 10% commission inside if I would get a job. She would also include an extra twenty-dollar bill. Hazel sent me out all the time! Mom was very wise.

I did a Kellogg's Corn Flakes commercial and a Heinz soup commercial. My very first commercial aired on *The Ozzie and Harriet Show* and was for Listerine toothpaste. Geez, for the commercial, I just had to eat a candy bar, brush my teeth, and smile; how much easier could it be! For that job, I got to go to school on set with Ricky Nelson and be directed by Ozzie. Plus, I received a nice check and residuals.

My first exposure to ballroom dancing was in the fourth grade. I was invited to join a cotillion, a series of dances with instruction in assorted ballroom steps, manners, and etiquette. It took place in Long Beach, at Kay Carroll's Peppermint Playhouse. I really enjoyed it, particularly the square dancing and being able to lead the girls around in ballroom dances.

Then I was invited to Call's Fine Arts Center. At their peak, they had 11,000 cotillion students! Derrall and Chloe Call had built their own beautiful ballroom in Long Beach, California, and I joined one of their cotillions. They had a daughter my age, so they decided to form a class called the "Medalist". Students with interest and aptitude were taught advanced steps. They held an annual Ball where students were awarded trophies for passing tests for ten steps in each of seven ballroom dances: waltz, foxtrot, swing, tango, samba, cha-cha, and rhumba. We first earned Bronze, then went on to Silver, Gold, and Gold Bar.

This is where I first met Barbara Boylan, who years later would become my dancing partner on *The Lawrence Welk Show*. Barbara and I were dance students at Call's cotillion. We were both just twelve years old. She was a vivacious gal and a good dancer. While I was on *The Mickey Mouse Club*, Barbara and I were learning ballroom dancing together and were put together as a team by our teacher, Chloe Call.

Barbara and I became the first king and queen of the annual Call's Cotillion Ball. At the Ball, we would be called upon to do dance exhibitions. The Calls brought in outside experts for different kinds of dancing. Our first exhibition at the Ball was a tango choreographed by Jeff and Birdie, an eccentric dance team from Bakersfield. He was gruff and bossed her around too much for my taste, but they did give us a good routine.

When I was thirteen, I was sent out to audition for the stage musical *Peter Pan*, starring Mary Martin. I got the part of one of the lost boys. This was a Los Angeles Civic Light Opera production destined for Broadway. It later became a legendary show. I got to rehearse with the wonderfully charismatic Mary Martin, learn dance steps from famed choreographer Jerome Robbins, and act, sing, and dance. Except—one night Dad said, "Let's go to an Angel's baseball game." Attending that game changed the course of my life forever as reported in an excerpt below from an August 8, 1954, article that ran in *The Long Beach Press Telegram* entitled "The Angels Done Him In."

> "The Angels done me in," says Bobby Burgess. And he is right, they did.
>
> Bobby, 13, last year signed a contract to appear with Mary Martin in *Peter Pan*. He was to play the part of a lost boy, Curley, and in the role he was to talk, sing, and dance. His salary was to be $120 a week. The show was to open July 19 at the Curran Theater, San Francisco, for a five-week run followed by the Los Angeles Philharmonic and then, Broadway. Theater people said it might run as long as Mary Martin's *South Pacific*. It was Bobby's big chance.

Then Bobby went to see The Los Angeles Angels play the Hollywood Stars in a baseball game. To realize how important the game was, Bobby and his parents are strong Angels fans while his grandparents, who also attended the game, root for the Stars. The two families razz each other about their teams. But Bobby shouted so hard for the Angels that he "blew out" his voice. It did him no good because the Angels lost—a regular "skunk of a game," says Bobby.

The next day, hoping that no one would notice how hoarse he was, Bobby appeared for his third rehearsal with the *Peter Pan* company. He could only talk in a whisper and his singing voice was a "whispering croak". "As soon as they heard me, they called me in and let me go," says Bobby.

For the role, Bobby had survived six eliminations, the last one on the stage of the Philharmonic auditorium. He was told that 1500 boys tried out for the role given him—which he lost because of the Angels.

I was crushed, but if I had gone to New York, I wouldn't have gotten *The Mickey Mouse Club*. It would have led my life in a very different direction. I guess everything happens for a reason, and in my case, it certainly did.

But, I continued to do other fun things. I got to be on a float in the Pasadena New Year's morning Rose Parade—twice! During my childhood, my family would plop our sleeping bags on the curb New Year's Eve to claim a space to watch the parade the following morning. As an adult, I first got to ride atop a beautiful float called Stairway to Stardom for the Exchange Club. I had won a big contest for them on my way up the showbiz ladder. And the second time was when Lawrence Welk was honored to be the Grand Marshall of the parade. We rode on a beautiful float, both my then dancing partner Cissy and I, along with other Welk stars Norma Zimmer and Jim Roberts. I remember one eager local shouting up to Cissy, "Show us your money makers!!" Another person shouted, "A Mouseketeer? I thought you were dead!"

Nothing like having the wind taken out of your sails.

CHAPTER TWO

What's a Mouseketeer?

When Mr. Disney was looking for children who would star in his new children's series, *The Mickey Mouse Club*, he would take some of his executives around to the local elementary schools, and say, "See those kids over there, those are the kind of kids I want to be Mouseketeers, a word he had coined to represent his young cast members." He didn't want any slick, phony child actors; he wanted the kids next door. Of course, we had to sing and dance, but he wanted the kids at home to feel they could be Mouseketeers, too. Fortunately, I fit the bill.

My agent initially sent me to Disney Studios to read as an actor for "*Spin and Marty*", one of the serials to be on *The Mickey Mouse Club*. They said fine, but do you sing or dance? I replied, "That's mainly what I do." I just happened to have my tap shoes in the car, and my music. They told me auditions were at 2pm. I hung around to try out and tapped as fast as I could to "Blue Skies". Then they told me to sing. I thought to myself, what should I sing? I'm a dancin' guy.

So I sang a song called "Way Down Yonder in New Orleans", mostly faking the words. But I think what got me the job was I had a gimmick. Realize that over one thousand kids auditioned for *The Mickey Mouse Club*. My gimmick was a barefoot jazz dance to "Rock Around the Clock". It was 1955, the dawn of rock 'n' roll. I got the job. I love Mouseketeer Sherry Alberoni's (a 1956 second-season Mouseketeer) line on how she got her Mickey Mouse Club gig. "I tap danced and played the trumpet at the same time; almost knocked my teeth out, but I got the job." That one always makes me laugh.

I went through five auditions, traveling surface streets from Long Beach to Burbank because in 1955 there was maybe one freeway. One audition was for the producer and director, another for the choreographer, and another when they combined kids into different groups. Walt Disney was at one of the last auditions, but as was his style, he was observing the selections in the rehearsal sound stage from the rear. But the producer had warned us beforehand: "Be your best today because Mr. Disney is coming."

That first year, there were 24 Mouseketeers, but the audience really got to know the 12 roll-call kids best. We were divided into three groups when filming started. The Red team, comprised of the roll-call kids, worked on "Fun with Music Day", seen on Mondays, and "Talent Round-Up Day", seen on Fridays. At the same time, the Blue team of six and the White team of six were doing "Guest Star Day" on Tuesdays, "Anything Can Happen Day" on Wednesdays, and "Circus Day" on Thursdays. You know, I got to present my future Welk cast members, The Lennon Sisters, on *The Mickey Mouse Club* way back in 1956 on Talent Round-Up Day. Boy, I had a crush on one of them. I'm glad it didn't work out. She has nine children!

Once all of the 24 first-season Mouseketeers were selected, we were put under contract. Mr. Disney didn't let any grass grow under our feet and we soon made our debut as Mouseketeers, not on TV but at the opening of his new theme park, Disneyland. It was three months before *The Mickey Mouse Club* debuted on October 3, 1955.

So, on July 17, 1955, Mr. Disney got us costumed, choreographed, and ready to go. We came dancing out of The Mickey Mouse Club Theater in Fantasyland. Everybody loved that location because it was the only air-conditioned spot in the whole park. On that hot, opening day in July, many of the drinking fountains weren't working and the asphalt was melting. Well, we were melting too in our hot, wool Talent Round-Up outfits. We did roll-call for the first time. I jitterbugged with Sharon, although it was kind of difficult to dance since it was not a real smooth surface.

Art Linkletter, one of the hosts (along with Bob Cummings and Ronald Reagan) of the live Disneyland Opening Day TV Special, announced, "These are the singing and dancing children of Disney's new *Mickey Mouse Club* called the Mouseketeers." Nobody knew what a Mouseketeer was. But we got out there and sang, danced, and paraded down Main Street U.S.A. at what became our very first public appearance. One special thing I'll always remember about Opening Day is a story Sharon tells about Mr. Disney, who had a private apartment above the Firehouse in the park's Town Square. She remembers looking up at that second-story window where Walt Disney was observing his domain, and noticing a tear running down his cheek.

Selecting the adult leader of the show, kind of the father figure for all of us, was up to Walt Disney. James Wesley Dodd was born on March 28, 1910, but became well known to kids everywhere via his nickname, Jimmie Dodd. He was a wonderful and kind man. Jimmie was also a devout Christian, although he never foisted that on anyone. I did sometimes attend his Hollywood Christian Group where Roy Rogers and Dale Evans were also members, and his "Share the Blessings" brunches at Easter at the Beverly Hilton Hotel in Beverly Hills. Jimmie and his beloved wife, Ruth, never had kids, so I think we Mouseketeers were kind of their surrogate children. They had cats, and he was a huge tennis buff, along with being an accomplished actor and composer.

Before he got into television and came to *The Mickey Mouse Club*, Jimmie appeared in a number of motion pictures. His first screen appearance was in the 1940 William Holden film *Those Were the Days!* in a minor role. He also played the taxi driver in the MGM film *Easter Parade* starring Fred Astaire and Judy Garland. In addition, Jimmie had a small role in an early episode of *The Adventures of Superman TV series*, entitled "Double Trouble".

Jimmie appeared in many theatrical films in the 1940s and 1950s as well, often uncredited. Two of his films were biographies of baseball players: *The Jackie Robinson Story* and *The Winning Team*, in which future president Ronald Reagan portrayed pitcher Grover Cleveland Alexander. Jimmie had a small, but important, part in the Mickey Rooney hit *Quicksand*, and he also appeared with John Wayne in the film *Flying Tigers*.

I love the story on how Jimmie was hired for our show. He was on staff in the Disney Music Department at the time Walt was searching for an adult leader to appear as the "host" of *The Mickey Mouse Club*. The show producers knew Jimmie and felt he was the perfect choice as head Mouseketeer, but the final decision had to be Walt's. So they set Mr. Disney up! They brought Jimmie into Walt's office and had him play his guitar and sing "The Pencil Song", his original composition. Jimmie's outgoing, friendly personality made a great impression. When he left, Mr. Disney turned to his executives and said, "I think I've found the perfect choice as the lead Mouseketeer, Jimmie Dodd." The setup had worked exactly as planned. And that's how Jimmie Dodd was hired.

Jimmie often played his Mousegetar on the show to his own self-composed songs. He wrote many musical pieces that were key to the show, including the "Mickey Mouse Club March", "Annette", the "Alma Mater" that closed the show each day, and "Encyclopedia", the song that taught a whole generation of kids (along with Jiminy Cricket) how to spell encyclopedia. He also wrote the theme song to the "Zorro" series among other musical accomplishments. Interestingly, Jimmie was also the voice of the animated character Bucky Beaver in TV commercials for Ipana Toothpaste, one of *The Mickey Mouse Club's* sponsors.

Jimmie Dodd was kind of like my "Mousekedad". People thought we were father and son because we had big smiles and big hair. But since "The Mickey Mouse Club" was in black and white, people didn't realize that Jimmie had red hair. So he wrote a special song for us called "Father and Son" where we sang, danced, and did vaudeville "schtick" challenging one another. I think that's my favorite episode. It ultimately became known as the "Bobby Show" because besides the first half of the show featuring my number with Jimmie, the second half featured me in a song and dance called "Shadow on the Wall" where I danced with my shadow. Except that it was not really my shadow but our show choreographer Tommy Mahoney dancing to my movements behind a scrim through which you could only see his shadow.

Another Jimmie Dodd specialty on the show was the "Doddisms" he created and wrote. They were friendly bits of advice and words to live by for kids. He passed on these words of wisdom in short segments as he sang and strummed his Mousegetar.

A very youthful looking man, everybody thought Jimmie was in his 20s or 30s while on the show. He was actually 45 years old when *The Mickey Mouse Club* started. He looked so young. Sadly, he did not live a long life. We lost Jimmie Dodd on November 10, 1964, when he passed away from a heart condition in Hawaii. He was only 54 years old. What a wonderful guy.

Our second adult leader was Roy Williams, also known as The Big Mooseketeer. He had been working at the Disney Studio for twenty-five years prior to his being drafted to appear on *The Mickey Mouse Club*. He was originally hired in 1930 as what was called "a gag man", supplying funny bits to be used in Disney cartoons. He later developed story ideas for Disney and designed over 100 insignias for the U.S. Armed Forces during World War II. However, no doubt Roy's greatest contribution to Disney (and one for which he was not compensated) is being credited with designing the mouse-eared hats worn by the Mouseketeers on *The Mickey Mouse Club* that have indeed become one of Disney's most iconic products ever.

Roy was such a character and a great artist. We Mouseketeers would make squiggles on blank easel paper, and he'd make cartoon drawings out of them. Plus, we had a lot of fun with Roy. During the summer months we'd often be invited to big bashes at his home, where we'd splash around in his Hawaiian-styled swimming pool (that he had dug himself!) with an island in the center. Roy passed away in Burbank, California, on November 7, 1976, at the age of 69. He and Jimmie both were posthumously named Disney Legends in 1992.

Disney Studios back then looked very much as it does today—a college campus lined with trees, two-story buildings, and lots of grassy areas. Even little real "Disney-like" squirrels live on the property. Two of its main buildings are the Animation Building and, across from it, the Studio Theater. It was in the theater where they put the "Mousekemoms". No showbiz, pushy moms were allowed on set. When a cute, popular roll-call girl's mom sat on the casting director's lap that first year to get better parts for her daughter, her little darling was soon let go. Those dedicated moms would spend hours playing cards, watching the latest cartoon features being dubbed and mixed, or knitting.

Cubby's mom, Zimmie, knitted Tommy, Cub, and me matching red, white, and blue sweaters. Close by the theater was the Studio cafeteria, known for its delicious food. I especially liked their breaded veal cutlets. Attached to one side of the cafeteria was a walled-off section that was no man's land, or no Mouseketeer's land. That was the Coral Room where the executives and Walt Disney ate. On the north side of the cafeteria was a big lawn, and that's where we'd play baseball or football. Ping-pong was big then also, with tables set on the terrace beside the cafeteria.

But after lunch, it was back to work and back to the Little Red Schoolhouse where we learned our lessons. The Studio had a "mouseke-production line" going by dividing all the Mouseketeers into three teams: one team would be filming, one rehearsing, and one going to school. The Little Red Schoolhouse was a red-painted trailer that sat outside our sound stage. There actually were two trailers, but mine had the primo teacher—Mrs. Seaman. She was a wonderful lady, and a great educator. She taught algebra, typing, and music history; but my favorite subject was Spanish.

Mrs. Seaman made all of us in her class speak Spanish to one another, and to this day I'm Roberto to many of the Mouseketeers, and they're Susita (Sharon), Tomas (Tommy), Darlena (Darlene), and Anita (Annette). Other Disney actors who were working on the lot also shared our classroom, including Tommy Kirk who starred in many Disney films at that time. For some reason, he only wanted to speak German. So Mrs. Seaman switched gears and taught him Deutsche.

Working, of course, was our main endeavor at Disney. *The Mickey Mouse Club* was filmed on Sound Stage One, a big, cavernous place with a flashing red light on the outside which meant "don't come in, we're filming". As you stepped in (when the red light was off), there was the prop table, and across the front of the stage was our huge blue Mouseketeer curtain with large heads of a boy and a girl wearing ears. The curtain is actually still in good shape all these years later.

Next door were two more sound stages, in one of which I remember watching them film the movie *Old Yeller*. I was recently honored to speak for the Mouseketeers when Stage One was re-dedicated by Disney CEO, Robert Iger, and named "The Annette Funicello Stage" to honor her memory.

There were 24 Mouseketeers cast for the first season of the show, and over the course of three seasons, a total of 39 kids became Original Mouseketeers. Seven of us appeared on roll-call every day throughout the entire *Mickey Mouse Club* run. It was Cubby and I, for the boys, and Annette, Darlene, Karen, Doreen, and Sharon, for the girls.

These are the original Mouseketeers who appeared on the series throughout its run:

> **Sharon Baird**, a great tap dancer, became my little pal. We first got together doing a number called "The Shoe Song" in the first season on "Fun with Music Day" and became jitterbug partners ever after. Our "Mousekedance" was a specialty number and staple of all future live performances. Sharon went on to appear in many Disney live-action shows in animal costumes (because of her 4'9" stature) and in commercials and character road tours.
>
> **Cubby O'Brien** was our great drummer. His dad was a well-known drummer and taught Cubby from the time he was old enough to hold a pair of drumsticks. Beyond *The Mickey Mouse Club*, Cub went on to play for many nightclub stars like

Shirley MacLaine and Bernadette Peters, is heard on all of the Carpenters' recordings, and drummed for many Broadway shows. Cubby and I were the only two Mouseketeer boys on roll-call for the show's entire run.

Tommy Cole was our boy singer. Although a three-year cast member, he joined roll-call the second year. When he realized being upped to the roll-call would require more tap dancing on his part, he frantically took lessons to make the grade. Tommy was also one of our top schmoozers when it came to dealing with the Disney "Mouseka-executives". He became a famous Hollywood makeup artist, winning an Emmy Award for his work. Tommy also worked for several years as our makeup artist on *The Lawrence Welk Show*.

Lonnie Burr was our intellectual Mouseketeer, graduating early from Hollywood Professional School and then UCLA. He did not appear on roll-call in the third year because he had injured his knee.

Doreen Tracey was our character, always funny and a little eccentric, but warm-hearted. In her post *Mickey Mouse Club* years, she entertained the troops in Vietnam with her singing and dancing act. She naughtily posed for a few men's magazines and ultimately went on to a career as an executive at Warner Bros. Studios.

Karen Pendleton was our little darling, blessed with that semi-hoarse voice, and famous for her rolled, blonde curls. She was the youngest Mouseketeer and was often paired in song and dance with Cubby.

Darlene Gillespie was to me the most talented all-around Mouseketeer. She sang with so much heart, could dance ballet and tap, and was even quite a comedienne. Her "Corky and White Shadow" series on the show was a big hit as well. Darlene went on to a country music recording career, but ultimately followed a completely different course becoming a surgical nurse.

And, of course, no one can forget **Annette**, who became the darling of *The Mickey Mouse Club* and our most popular Mouseketeer.

The balance of our first season troupe of mice were:

16 Ears and Bubbles

- Nancy Abbate
- Billie Jean Beanblossom
- Dennis Day
- Mary Espinosa
- Bonni Lou Kern
- Mary Lynn Sartori
- Bronson Scott
- Michael Smith
- Mark Sutherland
- Don Underhill
- Johnny Crawford
- Dickie Dodd
- Judy Harriet
- John Lee Johann
- Ronnie Steiner

Three original Mouseketeers that were only on one season each went on to become famous in their own right. Paul Peterson lasted only two weeks as a Mouseketeer. He couldn't contain his enthusiasm for the job and was found climbing the ladders to the catwalks on the set and mixing colors in the Ink & Paint Department. He got fired. However, he went on to a successful career appearing on *The Donna Reed Show*, in movies, and is now an advocate for children in television and motion pictures.

Johnny Crawford was a Mouseketeer the first season only. I don't know if it was because of his stutter, but his contract wasn't picked up. He went on to appear as the son on the popular TV series, *The Rifleman*. Eventually, he formed his own vintage-themed orchestra and makes appearances in cities throughout the United States.

Don Grady was another one-year Mouseketeer who went on to star in TV's *My Three Sons*. After acting for many years, he turned to his first love, music, and worked for many years as an arranger and composer for movies and TV.

That first year, I was so glad to have the Mouseketeer job, I danced with enormous and over-enthusiastic energy. We only filmed three seasons, but the third season was cut in half and a fourth season of new shows was created. By the third season, I had matured and finally grown into my gawky body and my big hair that always got messed up because I had to wear my mouse ears. That brings up the hat story!

We boy Mouseketeers were very proud of our '50s pompadours. But Gertie, our wardrobe lady, wanted those mouse-eared hats to show. She would put them on the front of our foreheads, but the minute she left, back they'd go, especially for me, Tommy, and Lonnie, so that our hair would poof out in the front. Cubby never had that problem because he had a flat top. And if you lost your Mouseketeer ears, you were docked $50.00.

I almost lost mine one time when the Mouseketeers appeared in front of 40,000 kids at the Oklahoma State Fair. It was windy that day and our black ears had turned to brown because of a dust storm. After our performance was finished and we clambered onto the bus, we started leaning out the windows to sign autographs. A teenage boy grabbed my ears and ran through the crowd. Fortunately, our heavy-set casting director, Jack Lavin, who was chaperoning us, jumped off the bus and tackled the boy. I got my ears back and saved myself fifty bucks!

On *The Mickey Mouse Club*, everyone wanted to have as much screen time as possible. So if the director asked, "Can anyone do such and such?" we'd all raise our hands, and say yes to almost anything. I did say yes once too often! I ended up having to learn to ride a unicycle for the Wednesday "Anything Can Happen Day" opening. How did I do it? The Disney people sent a circus performer to teach me in the driveway of my home in Long Beach. I only had to learn to ride forward, but then when I was scheduled to film they said, "And oh, by the way, you have to juggle at the same time." Whoa! I was determined not to let them down, and I didn't. It was one of the most fun things I did on *The Mickey Mouse Club*.

We had two great directors on the show. The first year was Dik Darley, a very thin, very capable man who was on the quiet side. All the girls loved him, especially Mouseketeer Sharon who had a major secret crush on him. He educated us about lighting. One of the things we learned was how the big central arc was spotlighted on us when we were performing. Occasionally, a certain Mouseketeer would move into the central arc to try to throw a shadow on the rest of us as we performed!

The second and third season, here comes Sidney Miller, ex-vaudevillian and former partner of Donald O'Connor on *The Colgate Comedy Hour*. Schtick, and lots of it, from Sidney! He did funny things, like puffing away at multiple cigarettes in his mouth with his glasses askew. He directed another of my favorite *Mickey Mouse Club* segments called "The Silent Movie". I was a robber at a carnival, and I put on a cotton candy beard. Just at the wrong time, I sneezed as part of the gag, and I was discovered when the cotton candy beard flew off. Then the Keystone Cops chased me.

Our third assistant director at that time was Ron Miller, who would summon us from the Red Schoolhouse for filming and play sports with us on the grassy field next to the commissary. He was married to Diane Disney and went on to become the CEO of the Disney Company for several years in the early 1980s.

Dancing, of course, was my forte, and I loved working with the people who taught us our routines. Our first year choreographer was Burch Holzman, later Burch Mann, who had a dancing school in Alhambra, California. Numerous Mouseketeers studied with her there. She later had her own folk dance company in Utah. She was a wonderful lady who specialized in tap. Then came Tom Mahoney. He was a jazz dance guy, and a character in his own right. He taught us well and after a while Sharon and I got to choreograph our own jitterbug routines.

We Mouseketeers had a lot of fun, but we also had to adhere to very strict rules that were set forth for all children who were employed in television and films. For example, we had to go to downtown Los Angeles to the school district office to get our child's work permit. We couldn't be biting our fingernails and we had to look calm like we were not going crazy from being overworked. They'd say, "Let me see your fingernails," or "Are you nervous?" And every six months our contracts could be renewed or dropped. So when renewal time came around we performed at our very best and were on our best behavior.

We also had to put 25% of what we earned away because of the Jackie Coogan Law, a government regulation that protected a portion of the salaries we received. So when I left Disney, I got a nice little sock of cash. My mom and dad saved every penny for me. Some of the Mousekeparents used their children's money to buy houses or put in swimming pools, but not the Burgesses.

One of the most amazing things about working at the Disney Studio during those years was the presence of Walt Disney himself. I would see Mr. Disney walking down Mickey Avenue or Dopey Drive, the main intersections at the studio, usually with his head down deep in thought. He wanted us Mouseketeers to call him Uncle Walt, but we '50s kids had respect for our elders. In 1955, Disneyland was opening, *The Mickey Mouse Club* and the *Disneyland* TV shows were in production, the animated feature *Lady and the Tramp* was being dubbed, and *Sleeping Beauty* was being created; so he had a lot on his mind. To us he was like a school principal. You just didn't run up to him and say "hi", although I suspect he would have smiled and offered us a pleasant "hello" in return if we did.

In fact, Mouseketeer Sherry Alberoni, who joined *The Mickey Mouse Club* in its second season and who I worked with often during our adult years, once encountered Mr. Disney as she walked along one of the Studio streets. He looked down at the then nine year-old little girl and said, "Hi, Mouseketeer Sherry." Of course, she was thrilled that he knew her name and immediately went into the studio theater to tell her mom, who remarked, "Honey, you have your name shirt on!"

One of the key reasons Walt Disney even created *The Mickey Mouse Club* was to help finance Disneyland. After Mr. Disney had cashed in his life insurance policies and mortgaged his house, he still needed money to finish the park. He went to the ABC television network to make a deal for help with the financing. They asked him to create and produce quality television shows for the network and they in turn would make a $500,000 investment to subsidize Disneyland's construction.

And so was born *The Mickey Mouse Club*, along with a weekly anthology series called *Disneyland* (what better way to promote the new park!). *The Mickey Mouse Club* was an ABC-TV ratings winner right from the first episode, as was the *Disneyland* series. It only took a short time for Mr. Disney to pay ABC back in full for their investment. In fact, ABC is memorialized at Disneyland, with four windows on Main Street, U.S.A. dedicated to the network. All four can be seen above the Candy Palace. They read: ABC, ABC Typing, Acme Business College, and ABC Shorthand.

Although Mr. Disney was busy with so many projects, we'd often see him in the back of our soundstage watching us film. He watched our dailies every day, and would share his ideas for the show. Once, when I was exploring the Animation Building, I glanced down a long hall to his office where I saw the seven little dwarf Oscars behind his desk that were given to him for his work on *Snow White and the Seven Dwarfs*, the first full-length animated film. On the way out, there was an easel, and on it I discovered I was storyboarded like a cartoon. There were sketches of Sharon and me jitterbugging with ears, teeth, and dust clouds in a number I knew would be coming up the next day. Yes, he was that involved with our show.

I loved seeing Mr. Disney and I would often sneak into the soundstage next door where he would film his intros for the *Disneyland* show. It was completely dark, and I'd watch this legend reading his cue cards with such natural warmth, just like he was somebody's favorite uncle.

I even got to personally work with Mr. Disney on an intro. I did a segment with him to introduce a movie then in the works, *The Rainbow Road to Oz* (from the famous Oz series), that was to star many of the Mouseketeers, including myself. He knew his lines, I knew mine, but at one enthusiastic moment, he hit me in the stomach flathanded. It knocked the wind out of me. I'm sure it was an accident, or done to emphasize a point, but I remember that incident to this day. Oh, and by the way, the Oz project never got off the ground.

But what a creative, innovative genius Walt Disney was. And what a privilege it was to have known him. His legacy lives on in his theme parks, animated films, television shows, and in the lives of all the people he touched. He was a true American original.

CHAPTER THREE

We're a Hit!

Variety is the bible for daily show business news. When *The Mickey Mouse Club* made its debut on October 3, 1955, its review of the show sent Mr. Disney, the executives, crew, and us Mouseketeers into the stratosphere. Here are excerpts of what they wrote:

> There's never been anything like *The Mickey Mouse Club* to hit television. There's enough here to keep the kiddies in every household glued to their sets most every afternoon. Jimmie Dodd and the kids are certainly finds—finds in the sense of talent in that every one of them can sing and dance and in tandem, they're great. About the best of the four segments on the preem show was the "What I Want to Be" serialized stanza, with the career kickoffer dealing with airline pilots and hostesses. *The Mickey Mouse Club* should have no trouble at all knocking the pants off the competition in the 5-6pm time period. It's the kiddies who rule the television tuners at that hour, and it's a good bet they'll insist on ABC, which should make Disney, ABC, and a host of sponsors quite happy.

From the *New York Daily News*:

> ABC-TV's *Mickey Mouse Club* is a smash box office hit, no doubt about that.

Syndicated columnist John Crosby wrote:

> The filling of five hours a week of entertainment is a massive enterprise which only the Disney empire could contemplate with equanimity. It's been tackled with great ingenuity...the show is studded with tidbits designed to enrich little minds. The cartoons from Mr. Disney's vast treasure trove are enchanting and many other features are good, clean, fun.

And those were just the tip of the iceberg of a long list of glowing reviews of the show. Before long, fan mail for the Mouseketeers began to pour in to the Disney Studio, and as time went on, thousands upon thousands of letters arrived every week, each addressed to a favorite Mouseketeer. I certainly got my share, but truth be told, Annette held the record for *Mickey Mouse Club* fan mail. Walt Disney had personally discovered her in her dancing school's production of "Swan Lake" at an outdoor theater in Burbank. Mr. Disney saw something special in her that night, and he personally selected her to be a Mouseketeer. In fact, Annette was the 24th and last Mouseketeer chosen that first year.

Italian was big in 1955, with stars like Gina Lollobrigida and Sophia Loren, so Funicello fit right in with this '50s craze. At one point Annette wanted to change her name thinking it was too ethnic, but Mr. Disney said, "No." He knew that once people got to know the name Funicello, they would never forget it. He was right.

But who really discovered Annette? The audience! Her charisma came across that television and every young boy wanted to marry her. She has even said, "I'm not the best singer or dancer on *The Mickey Mouse Club*." But she became our breakout star. It started when she was picked to step out from behind the ears to do a series called "Adventures in Dairyland". I was up for the part of her adventurous other half, but it went instead to "Spin and Marty's" Sammy Ogg. But I did have fun dubbing "Boys of the Western Sea", a Danish film Disney had acquired.

With each new season of *The Mickey Mouse Club*, you could watch Annette go through adolescence right before your eyes! I loved being her dancing partner on television and on tour, maybe because I was the tallest, and dancing to "Annette" written by Jimmie Dodd. We'd sometimes practice our lifts in the studio theater, but she was so feminine, she had hardly any strength in her arms. I tried an overhead lift to the shoulder. Uh oh. I accidentally dropped her to the carpet, and she just laid there, laughing hysterically. She was a warm, beautiful person.

Here's an Annette anecdote I almost forgot. I live in the Hollywood Hills, and one day as I was zooming down Nichols Canyon Road on my way to Hollywood in my red Corvette, I was pulled over by a policeman with radar who caught me speeding. After he approached and asked for my license and insurance, I noticed him staring. Then he said, "Are you Mouseketeer Bobby?" I said yes. And he responded, "Well, I won't give you a ticket if you tell me about Annette!" I did, and he didn't! I told him how beautiful she was both inside and out.

Annette always liked older guys. All of us Mouseketeer boys tried to get her attention, but she was more interested in Frankie Avalon and Fabian. We later learned her true secret romance was with Paul Anka and he wrote "Puppy Love" about her. She also had a crush on Zorro, Guy Williams. Walt Disney found out about this, and for her 16th birthday gift he arranged for her to guest star on the *Zorro* show and to have Guy Williams give her a romantic hug. She couldn't stop talking about that.

One day while in the Red Schoolhouse, we heard gravel being pelted against the window next to Annette's desk. She and a handsome young cameraman we named "Jack the Clanker" had a major flirtation going but, he being much older, Annette's parents Joe and Virginia put a stop to that. She eventually married her agent and had three children. I had a chance to be her date on a "Disneyland After Dark" TV segment in the 1960s. She always remained her friendly, down-to-earth self even after all the Disney movies, beach party movies, and international fame.

In light of *The Mickey Mouse Club's* popularity, the Disney Publicity folks decided it was time for the Mouseketeers to meet the fans. And did we ever, making special appearances at Disneyland, traveling locally throughout southern California to various venues and events, visiting many American cities, and even crossing the ocean to Australia.

Heading down the road from Burbank to Anaheim to perform at Disneyland was one location where we could frequently be found. After we'd finished filming Monday through Friday at the studio, we'd hop in our cars for the 35-mile drive to the park. We'd check in at City Hall and do multiple shows at a gazebo where the Pirates of the Caribbean attraction is today. After each show, we'd go out to Main Street U.S.A. for meet-and-greets with the fans.

Some days it was slow, so we'd compete with each other to see who had the wildest autograph. My Ys and Gs have "Z" Zorro signs on the tails, with giant Bs. Annette had hearts over her Is, and Tommy's is large and fancy. Over the years, we watched the park go from 22 attractions to over 60 today. As kids we Mouseketeers got to warm up the rides because we were given press passes. We'd have contests to see who could spin the fastest on the teacups.

Another Disneyland appearance was one of the best times I ever had. It was in November of 1955, after we had finished filming our first season, at an event promoted as "The Mickey Mouse Club Circus". We were to play two 75-minute shows a day through the Christmas holiday season. The Ted DeWayne circus troupe that had performed on one of *The Mickey Mouse Club's* Circus Day shows was brought in to teach us circus tricks. A big red-and-white tent was set up where the submarine ride is today, then called Holiday Hill.

The Mouseketeers did a "web", a long, climbable rope, and "swinging ladder act" dressed as Tinker Bells and Peter Pans. When they turned out the lights halfway through, we glowed in the dark. I was a web setter, stabilizing the rope for Mouseketeer Bonni Kern. During one show she slid down extra fast and I got her big toe stuck in my mouth!

I got to ride a baby elephant every day, and also a beautiful, black horse named Prince that I wanted to buy but he was too expensive to board and feed. Our mothers worked, too. Nikki Baird (Sharon's mom) and my mom were Chip and Dale in the opening parade, and were paid $6.00 each for two parades per day. But, as it turns out, Walt Disney wasn't too keen on this circus. He said, "Why would we need a circus when Disneyland itself is the attraction." He was right. We did not play to full houses and The Mickey Mouse Club Circus closed in early January 1956.

Often, world leaders were given personal tours of Disneyland by Walt Disney himself. In 1955, President Sukarno of Indonesia was coming to the park with his son. Two Mouseketeers were needed as escorts. Sharon and I were chosen. What an honor to be accompanying Walt Disney and President Sukarno and his son. We rode in a golf cart up Main Street, U.S.A. with a proud Walt and the president in the front, and Sharon, the president's son, and me in the back seat.

The studio kept us busy doing various benefits and special events. When there was a flood in Yuba City, they flew the Mouseketeers and their guardians to that northern California city to cheer up the populace. Yearly, we sang and danced at the St. Joseph's Hospital across the street from the Disney Studio, and we always performed for the deaf kids at the John Tracy Clinic in Los Angeles that was founded by Mrs. Spencer Tracy for her son who suffered hearing loss.

When we went to Australia in 1959 and 1960 with Jimmie and a group of Mouseketeers, I was 18 (and later 19) years old. All the Mouseketeers brought guardians, but it was kind of a breakaway time for me, so Jimmie and his wife Ruth were my "mousekedad" and "mousekemom". Ten thousand people met us at the Sydney Airport. Wow! We were bigger in Australia than in the United States. They tried to turn our cabs over, even tried to rip our clothes off, and when I performed, they screamed at my song and dance like I was Elvis. What fun!

We also had our own Pullman car when we went by train to a big Disney Fourth of July celebration in Evanston, Illinois, at

Northwestern University. Pillow fights ensued at night, but it was a pleasure looking out the windows seeing the full moon and, for my first time, fireflies.

I had a crush on Mouseketeer Cheryl Holdridge. She was our beautiful, blonde, outgoing dancer-singer who joined in the second year. She was always fun, and her mother was a former Ziegfeld girl and her dad was career military and called "the General". But on our 1959 Mouseketeer trip to Australia, she fell in love with Lucky Star, who was that country's teen Elvis. She later met Woolworth heiress Barbara Hutton's son Lance Reventlow. They ultimately married and moved to Aspen, Colorado. Their wedding was something else. It was held in a big Protestant church in Bel Air, and she was a gorgeous bride.

Mouseketeer Doreen was Cheryl's maid of honor. They were always best friends. At the reception, we met Cary Grant who was Barbara Hutton's husband at the time. But Aspen wasn't just known for its snow. Snow of another kind was rampant there, and Lance and Cheryl got involved with drugs and alcohol. Eventually, they divorced, and sadly, Lance was killed while piloting his own plane. Cheryl married twice more. With her third husband, Manning Post, she finally found the love of her life.

One day, Cheryl and I met in the aisle at a local department store after not seeing each other for a few years. I told her how much she meant to me and her fellow Mouseketeers. I spoke to her a bit about turning her life around. After she married Manning, she did indeed turn her life around and went on to become very active in charitable work and came back to join us Mouseketeers in the many shows we went on to do for Disney as adults. Cheryl had one of those smiles that lit up a room when she walked in. She passed away from lung cancer in 2009. I miss her very much.

Many famous people wanted to be Mouseketeers. Liza Minnelli has spoken of her desire to be an original member, and Paul Williams auditioned but didn't make the cut. Mickey Rooney's sons, Timmy and Mickey Jr., actually became Mouseketeers for one season. Jerry Lewis' son Gary wanted to be a Mouseketeer, but was eventually successful with his band Gary Lewis and the Playboys. Gary told people his favorite Mouseketeer was Bobby, and he invited me to his twelfth birthday party. We swam, dived off the high dive, and played baseball on his private baseball diamond with his dad Jerry as coach and pitcher.

We Mouseketeers also appeared on lots of Disney merchandising, and I'm proud to be on lunch boxes, paper dolls, and album covers. I guess they're collector's items these days. There are also ten selected DVDs from the show, and even a Disney treasure collection hosted by a big Disney fan, Leonard Maltin, who interviewed us for the piece.

Unfortunately, the Mouseketeers received no merchandising compensation. It was all part of our contract and we didn't know what we were signing; we were just kids. Our parents signed the contracts as well and most of them never read the pages and pages of fine print, either. Of course, we were just so glad to have a job! I was making $128.00 a week. That was more than my dad was making as a meat cutter. We loved what we were doing. It was more like play than work. Every six months, we'd get a raise. It eventually reached nearly $185 per week, including personal appearances.

At one point, Mr. Disney decided he wanted to make an Oz movie, as I mentioned earlier. The Disney Studio in fact owned the entire series of Frank Baum's Oz books, except for *The Wizard of Oz*. They planned to make *The Rainbow Road to Oz* as a feature-length film. Many of the Mouseketeers were cast in key roles. I became the Scarecrow, Doreen was a new character named Patches, and we had a dance together. Annette was the beautiful witch Glinda, and Darlene was Dorothy. We had no tin man, but Jimmie Dodd made a great Cowardly Lion. We had original music, great make-up, costumes, and sets. But unfortunately, for reasons unknown to me, the project was scrapped.

When it came to the Mouseketeers, I was usually always where I needed to be. But one day a photographer on the set noticed that Mr. Disney was nearby. Unplanned, he quickly got as many Mouseketeers and other *Mickey Mouse Club* cast members to gather around Mr. Disney as possible, shooting what has become an iconic photo of Walt Disney and members of *The Mickey Mouse Club*, sans Mouseketeer Bobby. Where was I? Right before the picture was taken, the assistant director insisted that our choreographer needed me immediately. Off I went. Oh well.

While I was on *The Mickey Mouse Club*, I actually got Barbara Boylan, one of my future dancing partners on *The Lawrence Welk Show*, on the Talent Round-Up part of the show. We danced a jitterbug and a waltz, and she was made an honorary Mouseketeer. Who knew what our future path together held?

Three seasons on *The Mickey Mouse Club* went by in a flash and before we knew it, it really was "time to say goodbye to all our company". One of the reasons the show didn't continue was because we grew up. We had all changed so much in appearance from when the show started in 1955. We were no longer kids.

On that last day, all the girls were crying. Sharon said she, Annette, and Doreen went through a box of Kleenex. I had had some truly memorable experiences, but missed my friends in my hometown. I had been at Disney from the eighth to the eleventh grades. It was time to move on.

CHAPTER FOUR

Where Do I Go from Here?

After *The Mickey Mouse Club*, I went back to my Long Beach Poly High School for my senior year in 1959. I graduated in the upper 2 percent of my class because of Mrs. Seaman's great tutoring. But my name had changed to "Mickey" as I walked down the halls. Everyone gave me the "business" because of my association with the Mouse.

Despite that, I jumped right into high school life. I became a freestyler on the swim team and joined the Drama Club. And at graduation I was voted "The Most Likely to Succeed". I followed up by attending Long Beach State College and joined the Sigma Pi Fraternity where I made life-long friends that I still see to this day.

But before I headed off to college, I got a call to audition for Edwin Lester of the Los Angeles Civic Light Opera for a major role in *Oklahoma*. I'd been under contract with him for the infamous *Peter Pan* fiasco some six years earlier. I brought my own pianist to the audition. Big mistake! She was an older lady from my aunt's Hard of Hearing Club. I started to sing "Kansas City", and all of a sudden realized she was not only playing the wrong chords, but had lousy rhythm.

You're right, I didn't get that featured role, but I did get to be one of the dancing and singing cowboys with a few lines. Inside info: we actually did "Gangnam Style", the same step that was such a hit by the South Korean singer Psi. Agnes DeMille had created this horsey step in the original *Oklahoma* production in the early 1940s.

When I think about my dancing style, I was very much inspired by Gene Kelly, Gene Nelson, and Fred Astaire. I even auditioned for Gene Kelly at MGM for a movie. I was surprised at how short he was. I did a few steps, but didn't get the part.

I met Fred Astaire at the taping of a *Hollywood Palace* television show. He was sitting in the front row of the audience, so I sat down next to him. I told him I'd read his book, *Steps in Time*, and asked about some anecdotes. He couldn't have been nicer.

I also auditioned for Robert Wise for *West Side Story* and read for him, but he said he was looking for a Bernardo and I'd have to wear brown contacts. Another audition was for the movie *Music Man*. But this was a heavy modern ballet role, not exactly my forté. They say you go to 15 auditions on average before you get a part!

Even though I didn't win every audition, I always kept practicing and augmented my tap with jazz with lessons from Donald O'Connor's choreographer Louis DaPron and his assistant Delores Blacker. I studied ballet in Hollywood with Eugene Loring and the School of American Ballet. I especially liked their men's class because of the strength of the steps, leaps, and turns.

But ballroom turned out to be my specialty. Just to give you a little background on this particular dance style, ballroom dance is partner dancing. Modern ballroom dance (what I do) has it roots in the early 20th century and became very popularized in the '20s and '30s in films starring the high-stepping Vernon and Irene Castle and then Fred Astaire and Ginger Rogers, perhaps the world's most popular dance pair. Ballroom dance comprises the waltz, tango, fox trot, and quickstep, among a host of others. All require specific techniques, tempos, vocabularies, and rhythms, which take time to learn. Although every ballroom dance style has its own particular aesthetics and rhythms, they have one commonality: a pair of dancers performs them all.

My all-time inspiration was the dance team of Marge and Gower Champion. I got to meet Marge later in life and she sent me many photos and memorabilia of her and Gower. I wanted to dance like Gower. I liked his masculine presence, the way he led, and his grace. I noticed that he didn't do big, overhead lifts in his dance routines. At one point, my *Lawrence Welk Show* partner Barbara Boylan and I found Gower's choreographer, William D'Albrew, in San Francisco, and flew up there so he could give us a few outstanding routines in the Marge and Gower style.

In 1960, Vegas called and I was hired as a dancer to back the then very popular music and singing stars, Louis Prima and Keely Smith. Back then Las Vegas was extremely different from today. There were very few hotels on the Strip. There'd be one hotel, then sand, a motel or shops, then a sandy desert lot. The place was run by the Mob in those days. You could get a great buffet for $2.00 at The Hacienda Hotel where the huge Mandalay Bay hotel is today. The expensive, gourmet restaurants were a long way off. And nothing was open late to get a bite to eat!

Lounge shows were big, as were French topless extravaganzas, no Cirque du Soleil. Downtown was quite off limits as it was kind of a rough, though flashy, area. The Rat Pack was big. Later, Liberace, Elvis, and other superstars got all the business. Of course, most people went to Vegas to "make their fortune" by gambling.

The show I was cast in with Louis Prima and Keely Smith was at the Desert Inn. It was patriotic themed to celebrate the presidential race of 1960 (Kennedy vs. Nixon). Myself, along with three other guys, sang and danced around Keely to a song called "You Gotta Use Sex", a spoof on the election.

That gig was an eye-opener. Every night I'd watch Keely down a water glass of scotch and then sing her charismatic heart out. All the showgirls and dancers were asked to mingle, or "mix", in the casino with the big gamblers after the show. And Louis, let's just say he had quite an eye for the ladies.

I'm a very "touristy" fellow and love to explore wherever I go. While in Vegas, I had heard that the Rat Pack would use the steam room at the Sands. So late one afternoon before my show, I ventured into the steam room and was amazed to be seated next to star entertainer and Rat Pack member Sammy Davis, Jr., who was telling great stories to a couple of toweled friends. I felt like a real Vegas insider!

And, of course, as a young man, I loved to date. I was a big fan of the Miss Universe Pageant held every year in Long Beach, California, my hometown. One year, while I was in college, out of the blue, I got a call to escort Miss Iceland to a dance. My sister Bette's good friend's mother was the head of the chaperones for the contestants. That was the connection. The chaperone in charge of the Icelandic girls became a friend, and invited me to escort a Miss Iceland again the following year. The third time was the charm, as I seriously started dating that year's Miss Iceland, who stayed on in the US until her Visa ran out and she had to return to her homeland.

Also during this third year, the head of the chaperones inquired if I could get twelve of my college fraternity brothers to be escorts to a dance for some of the other contestants. When I announced this at a frat meeting, the response was as if I had just made a final goal of a major soccer game and I was rushed as if it was a riot. The twelve lucky gentlemen chosen fulfilled their obligation, and I was the most popular guy that night at the fraternity.

I always had a lot of fun with my fraternity brothers, especially on some of our surfing and waterskiing adventures. I enjoyed surfing and got the bug after viewing the movie *Gidget*. I got my college pals together for some surfing safaris after purchasing one of the original Hobie surfboards, candy apple red, my favorite color.

Waterskiing was always on the top of my list for fun. After purchasing a ski boat that I named *The Bubble Machine*, one of my favorite spots to ski (besides Lake Tahoe) was in Long Beach up the cement-channeled Los Angeles River. It was always glassed off and someone had even put a slalom course up there. But don't fall. If you did, there was a foot of muck on the bottom. A few times when I wiped out, I got water in my mouth, and it tasted like oil from the local refineries and who knows what else.

We would have a lot of fun skiing past the local restaurants just south of the river. We'd entertain diners sitting out on the grass with tricks like one foot in the rope handles, squatting, waving, and arabesqueing. I guess I was entertaining even then!

We'd get our applause, then repeat our tricks for the folks on the deck of the *Queen Mary* that was permanently moored to the east. I would sometimes take my dates on a boat ride to see the skyline of Long Beach. On one occasion, Lynn Anderson, the country singer who was also on the Welk show, was with me and I hit a log and sheared a pin in my outboard motor (a shear pin is a safety device designed to cut off power in the case of a mechanical problem). I had to dive down to replace it as we sat dead in the water. When I came up after the task, Lynn was asleep. She didn't wish to go out with me after that! And that's when I bought *Bubble Machine II*, an inboard outboard with 350 Chevy engine—and no shear pin.

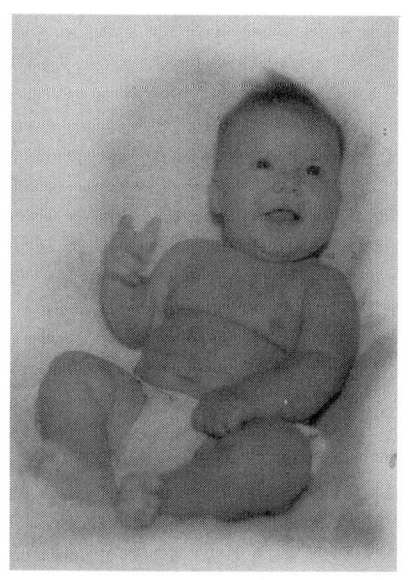

I was even smiling as an 11-week old.

Eating as usual at age 3.

My favorite sailor suit at age 5. Who let out all of
Mom's canaries from that cage behind me?

Bobby and Judy, who is my very first dancing partner, step out at age 6.

Age 7: We added the Hawaiian double gourd routine to our repertoire.

Time to go solo at age 8.

At 9, I was dancin' as fast as I could.

Favorite "glamour" shot at age 9, sent to casting directors by my agent.

Mr. Tap Shoes on the USS *Rupertus* at 11.

Four Burgess kids: Bill, Bobby, Bette, and Barbara.

Mom and Dad's 50th wedding anniversary: Barb, Bette, me, and Bill standing behind.

"The Angels Done Him In." I lost my voice, and lost my job with *Peter Pan* at 12.

Doin' my barefoot jazz dance at age 13 to get my job on *The Mickey Mouse Club*.

Mouseketeers at Annette's Birthday party.

Bobby, Sharon, and Lorraine on stools for interview.

Sherry, Lorraine, and Bobby in front of the Watergate Hotel.

Running for Black Bart for my Sigma Pi fraternity at Long Beach State in 1960.

CHAPTER FIVE

The Next Big Break

As a kid, I was a big fan of *The Lawrence Welk Show*. Before it went national, it was aired locally on KTLA, a Los Angeles TV station, from 1951 to 1955. I loved many of the performers on the show, too. Roberta Linn, the Champagne Lady who left the band in 1955 when she got her own show, was a special favorite of mine. I also watched every New Year's Eve never imagining I would be a part of it some day. The show was so popular locally that it became a summer replacement hit on ABC in the summer of 1955. The network then put it on the national schedule for the fall, and the rest is history.

I was also impressed with the big band on the show, and of course, Myron Floren, a lead musician who played the accordion. His fingers just flew across the instrument's keys making the most wonderful music. In fact, watching him inspired me to take accordion lessons, and for two years I studied. I even incorporated playing the accordion and tapping simultaneously. When I was eleven, guess who was the special guest at our Music Center Accordion Studio in Long Beach? Myron Floren! Little did I know, many years later he was to become my father-in-law.

Lawrence Welk, prior to his local and then national TV show, was never a famous coast-to-coast bandleader or recording artist. Born in the German-speaking community of Strasburg, North Dakota, he started his musical career at age 21 playing barn dances and fairs, and became known as what was called a territory band. He played every ballroom and every small town, so when he hit it big on TV, he had very special fans who had danced to him in the past.

He first put together a small band called The Hotsy Totsy Boys. Then they were the Honolulu Fruit Gum Orchestra, and finally The Champagne Music Makers. By the time he played such big cities as Los Angeles at the Aragon Ballroom, and Chicago at the Trianon, Lawrence had made many friends who were excited to welcome him into their living rooms on TV.

And how did I get my job on the Welk show? It started at the aforementioned Aragon Ballroom in Santa Monica, where Lawrence was appearing with his band. He had a weekly waltz contest and Barbara Boylan (who ultimately became my first dancing partner on the television show) and I had won one of the preliminaries. As I mentioned earlier, I had first met Barbara when we were both 12 years old and dance students at Call's Fine Arts Center in Long Beach.

But when it was time for the Welk finals, instead of being able to dance with my winning partner Barbara, I was whisked away to go on tour with Marie Wilson, a blonde bombshell, and protégé of comedian Ken Murray. When I came back, Barbara and I got together again at the Aragon Ballroom after Lawrence had recorded a song called "Calcutta," and he created a 13-week "Calcutta" dance contest. Barbara and I won it, and our prize was an appearance on the television show. We were both 19 years old.

At the time, Lawrence was also appearing at the Hollywood Palladium, a grand ballroom on Sunset Boulevard that he, his agent, and his producer had bought. Barbara and I went opening night, and stood in the front row wearing our red "Calcutta" matching outfits. There was another couple on stage from our same dance studio in Long Beach. But when Lawrence saw us, he dismissed them and said, "Bobby and Barbara, come up here and dance to 'Calcutta'."

We replied, "Mr. Welk, we have a new routine to 'Yellow Bird', your new hit." Of course, he invited us up.

We danced our hearts out and even included a nice "bird lift" at the end, and the audience gave us a big round of applause. Lawrence said, "Please come backstage at the end of the evening." We entered his dressing room and he invited us to appear on the television show the following week. We humbly thanked him for having us on the show, and added, "We heard you play a great version of 'Whispering' and that tune would work well with an English Quickstep." He responded, "How about doing a few steps for me?" We did. He especially liked a move called "the flicker", and laughed and clapped his hands. We won another week on the television show.

This was in 1961. We went week to week with the same approach until, six months later, he announced on the air: "Folks, Bobby and Barbara created a job for themselves, and you seem to like them, so we're going to make them a regular part of our show." Needless to say, we were thrilled. Thinking we'd be signing a contract, we were shocked to find out that Lawrence had no contracts! Twenty-one seasons just based on a verbal agreement. Try that in Hollywood today!

We also didn't have a choreographer on the show, so Barbara and I created our own routines. Actually, that was great for us because we could create the dances the way we envisioned them to the music.

Mrs. Boylan, Barbara's mother, was quite instrumental in helping us land this job. She was in constant contact with Ralph Portnor, or as we called him, R.P. the PR man. He was Lawrence's announcer and wrote a lot of his cue card dialogue. His tips were "stay humble and don't get the big head". And he was the one who told Mrs. Boylan about the Aragon, the Palladium, and the dates the Welk band played there. That's how we just "happened" to be there on those occasions that ultimately got us our job.

Barbara and I loved to go see dance performances, especially if they had a dance team or ballroom dancing. One of our idols was an adagio team named the Szonys. Francois Szony was partnered with his sister, but in later years when we would see him in Vegas, he would have different partners. He would be Szony and Clair or Szony and Agnese. Our first viewing of the original team was at Bimbos, a nightclub in San Francisco.

Barbara and I were sitting ringside next to the stage right exit. We noticed tension in Francois and his sister's eyes and in their dancing. As they exited, he was white-knuckling her hand. Obviously they were having a fight, and the audience could tell. From that moment on, I suggested to Barbara, and related to my future partners, that when we came off stage, we would not talk to each other for five minutes. Then we could calm down both emotionally and physically and respectfully have a discussion if everything didn't go as planned during the performance.

As for working together on our show, we learned that Lawrence had four basic rules. Number one: Be prepared. For the TV show, we did our dance about five times. We'd have three camera run-throughs, a dress rehearsal with audience, and the actual show with a new audience. At that first run-through in the morning, Lawrence would be watching the monitor in his dressing room, and he expected it to be as good as the TV show performance later that night.

Rule number two: Be on time. Lawrence had 45 people to pay and if you were late, it kept everyone waiting, and cost him money. Number 3: Don't put on weight. That camera put on 10 pounds, and he believed staying in shape was part of the discipline of being in show business. And rule number 4: No drinking on the job. He had seen many of the big bands, their leaders, or at least some of their best musicians lose their jobs and audiences over poor performances.

Lawrence loved to ask, "Are you happy in your chosen profession?" He certainly was, and wanted you to feel the same. In later years, he wrote several books. *Wunnerful, Wunnerful* was a New York Times best seller. Well-known satirist Stan Freberg established many of Lawrence's famous sayings such as "Uh-one and uh-two" and "turn off the bubble machine". Lawrence didn't like it at first when Stan made fun of his accent, but eventually came to embrace these trademark words for which he became so well known.

There were perks to being part of the Welk TV family. When I joined the show in 1961, our sponsor was Dodge automobiles. Everybody got a new Dodge to drive. Year after year, the band members would turn in their old keys and drive out with a new Dodge. A year after I joined, they changed sponsors. Then I got free Geritol, Sominex, Seratan (which is nature's spelled backwards), and oh yes, Poly Grip! But I'm a little older now, so I can appreciate those products.

Lawrence's Dodge auto plates read, "Ah-One and Ah-two" (spelled A1NA2) and he was a loyal man to his sponsors. He drove a Dodge until the day he died. He took Geritol and always smelled like Aqua Velva!

In 1964, Barbara and I, with Lawrence and the entire Welk band, were all invited to the World's Fair in New York. We played to huge crowds. But being the tourist of the group, I knew Disney was displaying attractions that were later destined for Disneyland. So I first got to experience It's a Small World, Great Moments with Mr. Lincoln, and The Carousel of Progress at this World's Fair. It was a dazzling preview of innovative Imagineering at its best, and to have memories of their first appearances was my personal privilege. To have Welk and Disney at the same venue was very special to me.

In my early years with the show, I still lived at home with my parents, But then I started getting tickets while driving my 'Vette the 35 miles to and from the studio. One afternoon Lawrence called me into his office and, as our musical father, asked, "Can I help you in any way?" "Yes, Mr. Welk, I keep getting speeding citations in my car." His reply, "You should move to Hollywood." I took his advice. No more tickets! Since I was 25, it was time that I move out, and I was guided by the maestro. I did my best all those previous years to keep normal by staying with my parents and driving in from Long Beach, but it was time for some independence.

I also prepared for my future in another way. I became a real estate investor. Because I didn't know if Lawrence would like a new partner after Barbara ultimately left the show, I bought my first apartment house. Each time I changed partners, I bought another apartment house. Luckily, he liked all my partners. And now I have four apartment houses. What a great way to make sure there is an income coming in, in case I ever broke one of my legs!

I like being a landlord, and am very hands on. As a landlord, many of my tenants become friends and make my apartments their home for years. But occasionally, being an apartment owner has its dark side. Three incidences come to mind.

My dad managed one of the six-unit apartments. One fall, two young ladies moved in, but didn't pay the rent. Dad hightails it to the apartment. As he knocks on the door to collect, the two girls open it, then proceed to push him down the stairs. Dad wasn't hurt physically, but it sent him for a loop mentally for a while. That same night, in the middle of the night, they vacate, leaving a massacred rabbit on the rug. I had to put in a new carpet.

In another instance, two women rented a two-bedroom, one-bath apartment, and a week later moved in the brother of one of them who was also the other tenant's boyfriend. He was a drug dealer! In the window at night, he had a sign OPEN or CLOSED. Most nights it was open, and there was a constant stream of druggies up and down the staircase. Yes, the cops were called, and eventually I eased them out. They moved two blocks down the street, and a week later came back to the apartment house and robbed all the carports.

I remember when four collegians moved into a three-bedroom unit. Eventually, one by one, three of them moved out, leaving me with just one friendly frat guy who no longer could afford the full rent. So I said, "Why not find a new roommate and stay." He advertised on the internet and that resulted in a woman from Seattle answering the ad and moving in.

I have a "no dog" policy, but she brought along her large, black husky that barked at the other tenants and tried to attack them. Then she invited her boyfriend to move in and installed two large video screens in her bedroom. Why? Turns out she was a high-priced call girl, and advertising from my apartment! Now my original friendly college guy is freaked out and he moves, leaving me with only this woman living there. One night while checking my apartment house, I see her leaving for work. Her boyfriend shouts, "See you later, Inga," not the name I was told was hers. Wearing a short black wig, skin tight shorts, sparkly blue dress, and platform shoes gave her the look she was desiring. "Inga" and her boyfriend stayed three months without paying rent. I had to get a lawyer and go to court to get them out.

Being a landlord obviously has its ups and downs. Despite the stories above, most of my years as an owner of several apartment houses have been great and I've made a lot of new friends.

CHAPTER SIX

The Welk Family

The Lawrence Welk Show had a large cast of performers. A number of them, like myself, stayed with the show for a long time while the tenures of others were shorter. Some of my co-musical family members included:

The Lennon Sisters were chosen for the Welk show when their oldest sister Diane told Larry Welk, Lawrence's son who went to school with her, about her singing sisters. He arranged for them to sing for Lawrence at his house. Lawrence loved their close harmonies, and put them on his Christmas show, always his highest rated show of the season. The audience reaction was unanimous. They loved them and watched them grow up on TV.

Sandi and Salli were a duo that auditioned for the show while students at Brigham Young University. They had worked as an opening act in Vegas for singer Jack Jones, and Lawrence Welk put them on the show. Salli eventually married our cowboy singer Clay Hart, and Sandi married her college sweetheart, Brent. Sandi and Brent have eight children and thirty-eight grandchildren now.

Guy and Ralna were the very popular singing husband-and-wife duo. Ralna was hired first, then brought Guy in as a guest on a Christmas show. Guy is from Elvis' hometown of Tupelo, Mississippi, and Ralna is from Spur, Texas. The audiences couldn't get enough of their romantic ballads, their friendly flirty patter, and their gazing into each other's eyes. They eventually divorced as many showbiz couples do, but continued to be friends, raise their daughter, and appear in concert together and on Welk reunions.

Tom Netherton was our handsome, tall, blond bachelor singer. Every grandmother wanted her granddaughter to marry Tom.

JoAnn Castle, our ragtime piano gal, also plays great accordion. When Big Tiny Little, the Honky Tonk piano player who appeared on the first five years of the Welk show, left, here comes JoAnn. What a character, loads of fun and talent galore.

Dick Dale was the bass saxophone player who Welk discovered could also sing. From Iowa, his boyish charm fit right in with the Welk image. And he could do comedy, too. He is the last surviving of the original Welk orchestra who came to Hollywood from the Midwest to do the local Welk Los Angeles TV show in 1951.

Jack Imel joined the Welk band right out of the Navy. He won something called the Horace Heidt (a famous big bandleader) Amateur Hour playing the marimba and tapping, the talent that got him the job on the show. Eventually, he became our associate producer and creative idea man. It was my privilege to work and tap with this good friend.

Joe Feeney, our Irish tenor, was from Nebraska and had eleven kids. His act on tour was always a big hit, and he was a great guy. He was known in the band for going over his time allotment during a show. If he was given a 30-minute spot, he'd sing for 45 minutes. We good-naturedly nicknamed him "Not Enough Songs" Feeney.

Arthur Duncan was the first African American appearing as a regular on a weekly variety TV show. He comes from a family of 13 kids. Art had tap danced all over the world, and his favorite thing to do was socialize with his fellow entertainers.

Ken Delo was brought to audition for the show by his friend Arthur Duncan because they had met and appeared at the same place in Australia. Ken was very versatile. He was a fine singer, emcee, writer, and comedian. We were good friends. He introduced me to the Pina Colada (uh oh).

Norma Zimmer was our Champagne Lady, and a lady she was. She thrilled her audiences with her beautiful soprano voice, but off stage she was a fun, down-to-earth gal. Before Welk, she did voice background singing and is the opening soloist over the credits in the Disney classic animated film, *Cinderella*. She loved to ski and had a home in Park City, Utah. She was also an accomplished painter.

Jimmy Roberts was Norma's singing partner, but could also stand on his own as a soloist. He had been the lead singer in Hollywood area nightclubs and theaters for years when Lawrence discovered him.

Buddy Merrill, the guitarist, joined the band in the 1950s, and then joined the armed forces. He reunited with the band after his service. I could be found skimming along the water behind his boat on his many trips to Emerald Bay in Lake Tahoe, where I learned to water-ski.

Mary Lou Metzger sang and danced on the show. She started her career traveling with a road tour version of *The Music Man* as the little girl Amaryllis, then came out to California after finishing college in Philadelphia. She auditioned for Welk and was hired. She originally did the Boop-Oop-A-Doop singing style that was reminiscent of Betty Boop cartoons, with the Dixieland group the Hotsy Totsy Boys, on the early Welk TV show. She went on to form a trio of Sandi, Gail, and Mary Lou, and teamed up with Jack Imel for singing and dancing sketches. She is now the primary host of the Welk re-runs and actually runs the Lawrence Welk office.

Anacani (Anacani Maria Consuelo y Castillo Lopez Cantor Montoya—that's a mouthful!) was our singer of Mexican descent and she sang in both English and Spanish. In either language, Anacani spoke in one universal language, music, along with youth, beauty and warmth.

Barbara Boylan. I was lucky. I had three outstanding dancing partners on the show. Barbara Boylan was my original partner and the girl next door. She appeared with me on the Welk show from 1961 to 1967 before she left to marry Greg Dixon of the singing quartet the Blenders, the show's four-man collegiate group. Barbara and I learned to ballroom dance together and had dated, but eventually were just great friends. She has two children and is today a grandmother of four. She taught dance for many years and lives in Denver, Colorado. When I was searching for a new partner in 1979 after my second partner Cissy King left, Barbara came back and did eleven television shows with me, and was better than ever. We brought back the "Best of Bobby & Barbara" and even added some new routines.

Cissy King joined the show as my second dance partner in 1967 after Barbara left to get married and stayed with the show until 1978. An accomplished dancer since she was a toddler, Cissy, with her brother John, had participated in the National Ballroom Dancing Championship multiple times. Cissy became one of the most popular performers on the show.

Elaine Balden (Niverson) was my third partner, after Cissy left. She was with the show from 1979 to 1982. I met Elaine when she was sent by a dancing coach friend to audition for me. She married Welk director and cameraman Jim Balden, and they have two daughters. Elaine and I still appear together as dancing partners in "The Stars of the Lawrence Welk Shows" that tour the U.S.

And then there's **Myron Floren**. In my opinion, he was the world's greatest accordionist. He very seldom looked down at the keys when he would play. Myron's South Dakota farmer father bought him the button accordion he picked out in the Sears catalog, and Myron completely taught himself how to play it. As a young man, he gave lessons in the area. A young high school girl, Berdyne Koerner, was one of his students. During World War II, Myron toured all over Europe with the USO entertaining the troops. When he returned home, he married Berdyne.

Myron was our emcee and directed the band on our Welk Stars tours. He toured extensively himself on as many as 160 one-nighters per year. He was definitely Lawrence's right-hand man on tour, making sure everyone was on the bus, including the boss, and arriving at the gigs early to make sure stage, sound, and everything else was perfect for the evening's performance. His nickname was the Happy Norwegian. He was a great father to five girls, and wonderful husband to Berdyne.

Because Myron was a good friend, I gravitated to the Florens, especially to attractive little Kristie, the second of his five daughters—Randee, Kristie, Robin, Holly, and Heidi. She was nine years old.

As Kristie tells it, "It was 1960 and I was in the fourth grade when I first met Bobby. He is one of the friendliest people I know, and back then he was no different. He already had the low down on the band families and he loved talking to people. I thought it was so nice that on the Welk Christmas Show days, he took time to speak to all the wives and their kids. Of Myron's girls, I was the one taking dancing lessons, so Bobby asked me about my dancing. I'm sure I didn't say more than a few words, after all I was only nine and very shy. He was one of the grown-up men on the show!"

Flash forward eight years. I had broken my foot polka dancing at the Palladium and was solo in my boat on an excursion to Emerald Bay in Lake Tahoe. There, sitting on the shore was this cute teenager in a white knit bikini, and her sister. Yes, it was the Floren sisters, Kristie and Robin. I asked Kristie if she wanted to water-ski. She said she had never done it, but to her and my amazement, skied all over the Bay on her first try!

When Myron was presenting the Welk stars at the Inglewood Forum at the Myron Floren Extravaganza, a fundraiser for the heart unit at Centinela Hospital, I needed a date. I asked Myron, "Could I take your daughter Kristie to the Extravaganza?" His response, "Why don't you ask her." I did, and we had a great time.

Kristie recalled of that date, "Bobby looked quite a bit different to me from way back when I first met him at age nine. He was SO cute, had a huge sparkly smile, and loved to have fun. He was just that much older than me (10 years) that my friends were kind of in awe."

I asked Kristie out on a second date to attend the opening of the Lennon Sisters at the famous Coconut Grove in Los Angeles. This time I blurted out, "Do you cook and sew?" Her reply with a straight face was, "Why, do you want to marry me?"

It wasn't long before I was a goner. I'd call her every day when I was on tour and send funny cards or notes with romantic sayings. Besides her beauty both inside and out, Kristie's innocence attracted me. She was shy, but at the same time, made me chase her. And she came from such a wonderful, happy family, like mine, with parents who had been married for many years. She also had several siblings, just like me. She understood my work, and realized that I—like her dad Myron—would sometimes be away on tour. She loved music, dancing, and traveling, all the things that I loved. The perfect match.

We'd often go down to the local park in Whittier, where Kristie was attending college, and cuddle on a two-person swing under a flowered trellis, or carve our initials inside a heart in a campus eucalyptus tree. We had a favorite Chinese restaurant. We'd return every Valentine's Day for many years to re-carve our initials, visit Penn Park, and feast on Chinese.

After dating for a year and a half, it was time for me to ask for her hand in marriage. I had enjoyed dating throughout college and as a young adult, but at a certain point, I got "ripe". It was time to find the one. And she was right in front of my eyes. But first, I had to get Myron's blessing. According to Kristie, that was not going to be a problem.

"By the time we began dating, my dad had known Bobby for eight years," she said. "Eight years of working on a weekly television show together and going on tour around the country several times each year while the show was not being taped. Sometimes, performers on tour away from home can be a bit naughty. My dad knew Bobby never had been one of those players. He welcomed him into our family with open arms. My dad had a special twinkly-eyed look and smile that was reserved for his daughters. He was never one for long-winded conversations. One time he gave me that look and asked if I was happy with Bobby. I answered yes. And that was all he needed to know."

After getting the okay from Myron, it was time for me to propose. I had to think of something unique and special. I turned to Disney! Nighttime at Disneyland is very romantic in many ways. I found the perfect spot. The Skyway ride from Tomorrowland to Fantasyland. There were twinkling lights below and "When You Wish Upon a Star" was playing. "Will you marry me?" I asked. Kristie said yes, and we kissed as we glided through the Matterhorn. She couldn't escape!

I then tried to think of a memorable way of giving Kristie her engagement ring. I took her to a nice restaurant near her college, and after dinner I ordered a bottle of Champagne and two glasses. She excused herself to go to the ladies' room. I slipped the diamond solitaire ring into her glass. When she returned, the waiter was pouring the bubbly. And then it happened. He stared at my fiancée and said, "Wait a minute. Is this young lady 21?" Kristie honestly answered "no".

How was she going to see the ring if she never lifted her glass? I had to fish the ring from the bottom of the glass, have a few sips of Champagne myself, and realize my romantic gesture had failed. But on our 25th wedding anniversary in 1996, I succeeded! Kristie was surprised to find a ring with four diamonds, one for each of our kids, at the bottom of her glass of Champagne!

Our wedding was quite an extravaganza. We were married on Valentine's Day, 1971, when I was 29 years old and Kristie was just 19. The church was packed with 1250 guests. The preacher was an old college friend of Myron's from South Dakota, Pastor Bjerke. After our vows at the church, we hosted a dinner reception for 650 inside the red-and pink ballroom of the Pacific Coast Club in Long Beach. Many friends and family members attended, along with many of the Mouseketeers and Lawrence Welk Show cast members.

In attendance were Annette and her then Hollywood agent husband Jack Gilardi, Darlene Gillespie and her spouse, Doreen Tracey and her date Bobby Diamond of *Fury* TV fame, Sharon Baird, and Tommy Cole with his wife Aileen. I had fourteen groomsmen and Kristie had six bridesmaids with her sister Robin as Maid of Honor. My lifelong pal, Mike Ryan, was my best man. Our white dinner jackets sported red bow ties and hankies and red carnations. The bridesmaid dresses were red velvet. Kristie was a beautiful bride.

From the Welk show, Norma Zimmer sang "Ich Liebe Dich" (I Love Thee Dear), by Edvard Grieg, during the church ceremony. We had a heart-shaped cake with a fountain in the middle. Joe Feeney sang "I'll Be Loving You Always" for our first dance at the reception. Myron read a lovely thank-you note Kristie had written to him and Berdyne. Lawrence Welk even attended and polka'd with Kristie while I danced with my mom.

Unfortunately, we also had some uninvited guests that showed up. Myron had been telling his concert audiences all over the United States, "Bobby Burgess is marrying my daughter Kristie on Valentine's Day. So if you're in Long Beach on February 14, come on by." This always got a chuckle in his act. But one week before the wedding, he used the same line while playing at the Downtown Long Beach Businessmen's "Good Ole Days". We had to hire security guards and cordon off the walkway into the church to keep the local fans at bay.

But all ended well and we danced the night away, then spent a week's honeymoon in Hawaii. For Kristie, her role had changed. She went from being a "band kid" to being a "band wife" in the Welk TV family. My role had changed, too—I was a husband!

CHAPTER SEVEN

Changing Partners

The Lawrence Welk Show made its national TV debut on ABC television on July 2, 1955, and was produced at the ABC studios at Prospect and Talmadge in Hollywood. For 23 of its 27 years on the air, the show originated there. The only seasons not produced at that location were 1965–66 and 1976–77 at the Hollywood Palace, and 1977–1979 at CBS Television City.

The 1965-66 season was taped at the Hollywood Palace since that was ABC's only West Coast TV studio at the time equipped for live or taped color production. Welk had insisted that the show go color in 1965 because he believed it was critical to the continued success of his program. Once a couple of studios at the ABC Prospect and Talmadge facilities had been converted to color in 1966, the show moved back there.

Lawrence was a stickler about taping our show. He never wanted anyone to stop while taping. If they did, he'd have to pay the cast and crew overtime, and he was of the frugal persuasion. If someone forgot the words to a song, he'd say, "Leave it in, it looks like live TV." He was brought up on live TV broadcasts before taping shows became the thing to do. Only twice can I remember us stopping taping.

Once we were doing an outer space number with dry-ice fog. My partner at that time, Cissy, slipped and disappeared into the mist and said, "I'm not getting up." The other time, we were dancing the Philippine folk dance, Tinikling, with the clacking bamboo poles. She got her ankle caught, started crying, and Lawrence stopped tape. The boss gave in only for emergencies.

Cissy was my second dance partner, and she was an outstanding dancer. We had a terrific act for twelve years and made many people happy. When I was looking for a new partner in 1967, and Barbara had left the show to marry, I placed an ad in the *Hollywood Reporter* and *Variety* to audition a new partner. I rented a studio and a myriad of girl dancers appeared. All ads read "Must Know Ballroom", but most would do their theater arts dances and then say, "Ballroom, just show me." Well, it is a studied art, and very technical, so I knew right away this was not the one when she'd make that statement.

The one audition I remember the most was this cute, perky girl from the Midwest. After doing some jazz, she ran to the side of the hall and bam, flip-flopped, cartwheels, and round-offs across the floor. Whew! When I tried to show her some basic quickstep, I don't think she'd ever danced with a partner, so obviously she didn't get the job.

Cissy was a different story, and she was my partner from 1967 to 1979. Barbara and I had competed in dance contests against her dancing brother John and his future wife, Kathy. Our dance studio, Call's Fine Arts Center, were rivals of the studio run by John's and Cissy's ballroom teachers in Albuquerque, New Mexico, the Vanderpools. I was asked to be a judge for a dance contest at the Hollywood Palladium, and that night is when I first saw Cissy King. Was this the sister of John King? I knew that Cissy, with her brother John, had participated in the National Ballroom Dancing Championship multiple times and that she was a terrific dancer.

My mind went into overdrive and I thought, "If I could dance with Cissy, I could combine my steps with the steps from the Vanderpool Studio, and have a new look and new direction." I auditioned Cissy who seemed to specialize in the standard, or smooth, dances, and was very good at lifts, as she'd been a gymnast. She got the job. We danced together for twelve seasons on the Welk show.

One of my favorite tour stories with Cissy was about an outdoor appearance at a county fair in Evansville, Indiana. At rehearsal in the morning, we put our music down on the bandstands, and the musicians, who were local, said, "We don't read music." I asked, can you play a waltz? "No." A polka? "No. We just play chords behind the rock group." Then I looked down and the piano player was missing fingers on one hand; he only had a thumb and pinky.

I quickly called the booking agent and he sent over the high school bandleader who played trumpet. We used their drummer and that was our "band". And then it started raining with 100% humidity! They put a low-hanging tarp over the stage. I was carrying Cissy across the muddy fairground to the stage, slosh-slosh, when the fair manager runs up to us and says, "There's a tornado coming, so we're cutting the rock band short so you can go on."

We do our act, have to cut the lifts because of the low overhang, and they've locked the gate to the audience, so no one can come up to dance the polka with us. Now the tornado can been seen on the horizon and the audience disappears and we disappear under the stage. Fortunately, the swirling cloud goes around us, and the manager, panicking, runs up again and says, "You've got to dance the act over again!" We're exhausted, but nobody saw it. They let the audience back to the viewing area and we repeat our act as requested. Finally, we're able to leave and the next day we head for the airport. But when we get there, they don't have our reservations. I call our travel agent and it turned out he booked us out of Evansville, Illinois. Unfortunately, we were in Evansville, Indiana, 100 miles away! Sometimes, nothing seems to go right.

Not going right can sometimes also be downright scary. During our time on the Welk show Cissy had a stalker. We noticed a guy in a black leather jacket on a motorcycle hanging around the Palladium parking lot some nights. Then one night he approached Cissy and said, "I'm Cary Grant and you're Doris Day, and we're meant to be together. You're my wife." She got out of there fast as I stood watching with my mouth open.

From then on I always walked her to her car. But unfortunately, it didn't stop the problem. We were filming at CBS, security is lax, and there he is again. Next, back shooting at ABC in Hollywood, he's rented an apartment on the street that leads to her freeway drive home. He stands outside watching and mumbling, waiting for her to drive by. Even though nothing physical happens, the frightened Cissy gets a restraining order and, fortunately for her, he disappeared from her life.

Another time I sent Cissy to the hospital. We were doing the show at the Hollywood Palladium right after the Emmy Awards had been broadcast from that same stage. What we didn't know was that the set decorator for the show had left several plexiglass panels on the stage. Clear ones. As I raised Cissy in the air for the bird lift in our "Yellow Bird" routine, I accidentally whacked her foot on the plexiglass, causing a gash in her leg with lots of bleeding. We immediately took her to the hospital for stitches and she was just fine. A fan magazine photographer who happened to see the accident happen followed us to the hospital. A story appeared in the tabloid the next month with a close-up of the cut.

Cissy and I danced in so many venues it's often difficult to remember them all. But one that does stand out was our appearance at Madison Square Garden in New York City. Lawrence was always reluctant to play New York City. He thought he could only get a really big crowd in the Midwest. Wrong. His manager booked him into Madison Square Garden in the 1970s, and he proceeded to fill the arena with a sold-out audience of 22,000 people. Of course, he was asked to return the next year and he did with the big band and played once again to a huge house.

For me, this engagement was memorable not so much because of the actual appearance but because of a few unforeseen incidences. First, the New York Musicians' Union "featherbedded" the boss. Lawrence was told he had to hire and pay an extra fifteen local musicians just to sit on the side of the stage. The union line was that Lawrence's 23-piece band was taking local jobs. Lawrence was very anti-union and this did not sit well with him at all.

Secondly, the stage itself was one of the worst. It was in uneven wooden pieces and had pits and rough spots here and there. Jimmy Roberts, our tenor, was introduced and walked out only to trip and fall flat! Cissy and I did our best to be smooth, and danced around the "pot holes" and splinters. And to top off the evening, Lawrence introduced Woody Herman's "Woodchoppers' Ball" as "Woody Woodpecker's Ball!"

Under almost all circumstances, having Cissy as a dancing partner was a fun experience. But she had one really bad habit and that was that she was habitually late…to everything. She became known as "the late Miss King" by the band. She had a real problem with punctuality. A couple of her classic excuses were, "I couldn't get here on time because a tree fell across my driveway and I couldn't move it." And "someone turned the water off in my house, so I had to go to my brother's house to take a shower."

A date in Oklahoma was the catalyst for Cissy being let go. She was running late for a date in Tulsa. She wasn't on the bus to the auditorium with the band, so she had hitched a ride with friends. She got caught in traffic, and actually got out of the car and started running toward the arena. We were in the opening number, no Cissy, so I quickly taught Mary Lou Metzger, a singer and good dancer, our "Jukebox Saturday Night" routine. Lawrence didn't notice.

Now it's time for our "Champagne Waltz". No Cissy. Lawrence calls me into his dressing room and says, "You need to find a new partner, or are you not man enough?" With that, I knew that "Bobby and Cissy", after twelve seasons on the show, were over. He also said that he'd like to try out three different women for the spot who would each perform with me on air. In that way, we'd be able to gauge how each appealed to the audience as well. I quickly got to work to meet the challenge.

My wife, Kristie, and I headed over to the Emerald Ballroom in Santa Monica to start the search. I noticed an all-American girl winning the Latin competition and booked an audition with her. She was not only a good ballroom dancer, but also an outstanding tapper. She was a little tall for me to do lifts but I could overcome that. As it turns out, she was not only dancing with her current partner and not seeking a new one, but was also in a romantic relationship with him. I couldn't overcome that. Strike one. But as an aside, she and her partner went on to win the United States Ballroom Latin Championship seven times in a row!

Next, per a request from me, the Fred Astaire Dance Studios sent over a beautiful brunette from Chicago, and after auditioning her, I think she might be the one. I put her on the Welk show and we danced a smooth fox trot with lifts. But when Lawrence called her over to introduce herself, her nasal voice and Chicago accent did her in. Strike two.

Next, I find a girl who is a "disco queen" and a really nice person. I put her on the show as well where we danced a polka and a 1970s disco. Unfortunately, the audience reaction was very mediocre so she too didn't make the final cut. Strike three. Time to step up the search.

Friends of mine from Houston, Texas, Robin Stockdale and his mom, were also two of my biggest fans. Robin recommended a gal who was the supervisor of the dance studio where he worked. Roy Maver, an international Ballroom Champion, owned this studio. So I start thinking that since I do my own choreography, if this girl works out, she'll bring all of Roy's neat steps to the team.

Kristie and I meet the girl, Elaine Niverson, for the first time at the airport. She stood outside baggage claim with her suitcase in hand and a large hat on her head. It was like something out of a 1930s movie. We take her to CBS, where the Welk show was currently filming, to audition for me. I have her do all the different ballroom styles and nod my approval over my shoulder to Kristie who is watching. I have Elaine sing and tap. I dance a rhumba with her on the TV show, she being outfitted in an appropriate costume for the number.

Unfortunately, that day Elaine has a terrible cold. She's taken antihistamines, so as we're dancing, her upper lip keeps getting stuck on her teeth. On a lunge, she gets her foot caught in her dress. Thank goodness it's stretch material and didn't rip. Afterwards, our wardrobe lady, Rose Weiss, comes up to me and says, "You're not going to have that girl as a partner are you? She's so stiff!" Well, Elaine was actually doing International rhumba correctly, but to Rose it did look odd. Despite the runny nose and the dry mouth, and catching her foot on the dress, Elaine came through with flying colors. But she wasn't officially hired yet.

Shortly thereafter, on tour with the Welk band (one of my last appearances with Cissy), I invite Elaine to see our show. She comes backstage and Welk puts her in dance position and twirls her around and does a few steps. His comment? "She lets me lead." So Elaine gets the job and Lawrence announces at the beginning of the 1979 season Bobby's new partner, Elaine Niverson. I guess number four was the charm!

We put an act together, and during our first summer we appear at twelve theaters-in-the-round, usually with Myron Floren as emcee and conducting the band, Guy and Ralna singing, us dancing, and one other act from the show. We do sold out business! And the secret the promoters know? Matinees and bus tours! Our older audience wants to see our show, have dinner, and be in bed by eight. Elaine is easy to get along with and is always on time. We finish out the last three seasons of the Welk weekly show.

If you've ever watched *The Lawrence Welk Show*, you know we always had very colorful and often elaborate costumes. But our wardrobes weren't made at the studio. Many times they were rented. One dress worn by my dance partner Elaine came from Western Costume Company. It was a vintage, ruffled tango dress, probably from the '20s, with the ruffle trailing behind like a train. I stepped on it! Now following behind, it looked like Elaine had a tail! I dodged it the best I could, because of course, the show must go on. We finished the routine and Lawrence said it looked like live TV, and would not allow us to re-tape (remember—it cost him extra money to do that!).

At our next personal appearance, a lady fan came up and said, "I saw you and Elaine the night you did the tango and ripped her dress when you stepped on it." I hope most of the fans watched my dance and didn't simply focus on the ancient torn dress. By the way, the tango is my favorite dance, followed by the swing.

Sometimes our costumes were not rented. We actually had to purchase them ourselves. Lawrence made us buy our band uniforms, so we ended up personally owning mustard colored coats, orange suits, red jackets, and more. Years later, when Kristie and I attended the ballet in Hollywood, I decided to wear one of these band suits. Never again! At intermission, I heard a guy whisper to his wife, "Only in Hollywood would you see some guy wearing a turquoise suit!"

Even though I may have had to buy some of my own wardrobe for the show, I did get to do my own choreography. My partners and I practiced two or three hours daily. We'd find a step, add a step, and have a combination. We'd get the theme about two weeks in advance, then we were allowed to suggest the music and create the dance. We'd request certain sets if possible and also tell our costumer our needs for dance clothes. If we didn't know how to do a certain dance, we found coaches who were experts in their fields to help us.

Laure Haile, of Arthur Murray Dance Studios, knew many vintage dances. Dr. Hall at USC was our folk dance guy. Louie DaPron, Donald O'Connor's choreographer, would help us in creating theater arts dances like a "Fred and Ginger" medley or a scarecrow dance. William D'Albrew, Marge and Gower Champion's choreographer, gave Barbara and me beautiful ballroom routines and even a cakewalk. Sheila Sire was a fine standard ballroom coach. All were very accomplished in their fields of dance and were always there for us when we needed them. But I had the ultimate responsibility for the choreography, and I loved putting my creativity to work.

Of course we were also not above "borrowing" a few steps, either. You see, all dancers have something in common. We're always watching other dancers. Well, there's a special reason for this. We steal each other's steps! I'm no exception. I love watching the old movies on television with Fred and Ginger, and Gene Kelly and his partners. One night I was watching an old Donald O'Connor movie, and he was doing a dance I liked so much, I didn't just borrow a step or two, I stole the whole dance! It was an old soft shoe from the 1930s, the days of old vaudeville, which called for a hat, a cane, and a little sand for a sand dance to "Two Sleepy People".

Sometimes we'd even steal a joke or two. One of my favorites jokes I "borrowed" was from Bud and Cece Robinson, a dance team that toured with Johnny Carson. Actually, Cissy and I were also lucky enough to make an appearance on Carson's *Tonight Show* when

Lawrence was a guest and he presented us to the audience. But when I attended Bud and Cece's show one night, I liked one of their best lines and revised it to work for Cissy and me. In the joke, I'd say, "I love ballroom dancing, but today's dancing is something else. Everybody does his or her own thing. The girl dances over here, and the boy dances over there. In fact, Cissy and I once entered a rock dance contest and were lucky enough to win it. Cissy was in Hollywood, California; I was in Oshkosh, Wisconsin!"

CHAPTER EIGHT

Lawrence Welk

Lawrence instilled confidence in me since he trusted me to do my own choreography. I set camera angles that were essential to how well the dance was enjoyed by the TV viewing audience. As I had taught a class at USC called Choreography for Television, I directed my own videos. I made suggestions on the Welk show on direction for my own dances by writing in angles for the director.

Like Fred Astaire, I preferred head-to-toe shots unless there was a need for close-ups of fancy footwork. So when I'd move to the side with a step, I'd have the camera "truck" to the side to follow my actions, and this all worked out well to create the vision I had in mind. For lifts, I liked one camera to dissolve into another to give the illusion that my partner was floating up to my shoulder.

Luckily, all my years at Call's dance studio gave me a great foundation for creating choreography and envisioning how it should look on the TV screen. During my years at the studio, I had to learn ten steps in each of seven dances to be in their medalist program. I passed tests for bronze, silver, gold, and gold bar, and received a trophy for absorbing all that knowledge which would serve me in my future. To dance in front of that great 25-piece Lawrence Welk band every week was always truly inspiring.

Occasionally on *The Lawrence Welk Show*, I got to dance with the ladies in the live audience. One night, a rather heavy-set lady came up to me, slapped me on the back, and said, "I want to dance with YOU." So she took me in HER arms! I had a nice, simple step to get started, "Ah-one and Ah-two" from side to side. We started dancing and I noticed the lady was giving me a rather unusual stare. So I said, "Is something wrong, ma'am?" and she answered, "Bobby, on television, it looks like you're a much better dancer!"

Lawrence Welk always enjoyed it when people from the audience participated in the show, like the dancing lady above. He respected his audience and one of his keys to success was playing what they wanted to hear or performing what they wanted to see. He would ask his parking lot attendant's opinion of the show the previous Saturday night, and would take his suggestions into the Welk meetings for the following week's show.

Lawrence's musical "sound" became known as "champagne music". The phrase was coined when he played the William Penn Hotel in Pittsburgh and someone said his music reminded them of champagne bubbles. Thus, "champagne music" was born. Along with that came Lawrence's famous champagne bubbles, necessitating the use of a bubble machine during shows. At first, on tour, the bubble machine would spew bubbles across the stage in front of the band during the opening of the show. Uh oh! Lawrence slipped and went down; so did I at one time.

For the television show, the bubbles were relegated to the rear of the stage to pop up from behind the bandstand to save us from a slippery floor. Uh oh! Now the violins, the bass, and cello people complained that the bubbles were warping their instruments. So, in later years, the bubble machine was placed at the side of the stage and the bubbles were filmed and super-imposed on the screen, affecting no one. In future years, Lawrence let me create the pop-fizz cork sound before he went on stage at the opening of the show on tour.

Lawrence Welk loved to play golf. He was always invited to the Bob Hope Desert Classic in Palm Springs and to the big Walt Disney World golf tourney in Florida. One of his only trips outside the United States was to Spain for a golf tournament. One time, when the show was filming at the Welk Resort in Escondido, California, we heard, "Hold it, would you let the boss play through?" The cameras were on us, but we were facing the foursome. Wouldn't you know it, Lawrence got a hole-in-one! We saw it, but unfortunately the cameras didn't.

Lawrence also loved to dance, especially the waltz and the polka. But he had the most fun jitterbugging to the big band. My favorite moves that he did were "snake hips" and "heel, step, heel, step, march, march" with that Welk smile while snapping his fingers. You could tell he was really digging the music when he launched into one of these steps in front of the bandstand.

When I joined the band in 1961, I didn't know how to do the Polish-influenced "Lawrence Welk-style polka". I was doing the American smooth style with a 1-2-3 hop. One day when I was trying to figure it out, it was Aladdin, our violinist, who stopped me and said, "Let me show you the Polish Hop." Jump, hop hop; jump, hop, hop. From then on, it was the Polish Hop I used in all my routines because it was flashier than the American style, and I knew that Lawrence preferred it.

Lawrence had many famous people on his show, and what fun it was to work with them. They would do their "act", then we'd all get to sing and/or dance with them. Some of the outstanding guests were Jack Benny, Henry Mancini, Bobby Vinton, Kate Smith, and Pat Boone. I had two particular favorites. The first was when Kate Smith was on the show; she sang her signature song, "God Bless America", with music conducted by George Cates, our musical director.

Kate had sung the song thousands of times, but George was rushing the tempo. She stopped mid-song at dress rehearsal with an audience in attendance and said, "George, this is my song, so you need to follow ME, not the other way around!" A sheepish George took the criticism, and this time eagle-eyed her instead of having his back to her, to Kate's satisfaction.

My second favorite was Jack Benny's appearance. It was a return favor as Lawrence had appeared on Jack's TV show. Lawrence gave him the baton to conduct the band. Benny waved the stick and the band fell to pieces in dissonant chords. Sheepishly, he turned to Lawrence, and the boss said, "You have to open the champagne bottle." So Benny, with a semi-successful cork pop, started up the band's big gag number to "Bye Bye Blues".

The number was a staple at Lawrence's appearances at the Hollywood Palladium where he would get a volunteer out of the audience to conduct. "Bye Bye Blues" consisted of various sections of the band rising and sitting while playing. At one point, Lawrence plops himself in a trumpeter's seat as he's standing up for a section solo and gets sat on when the trumpeter sits back down. That was always good for an audience laugh. Near the end of the number, the drummer accelerates until the orchestra is playing twice as fast with Benny looking frustrated. When the number was over, Benny says, with his chin in his hand and his elbow in the other, "WELL, THAT was an experience."

In the audience, Lawrence was proud to introduce various guests like Meredith Wilson when we did a salute to "The Music Man". For our Irving Berlin show, Lawrence announced, "We have one of our greatest song writers of all time with us tonight, Irving Berlin," although he mispronounced the name as Irvin Berlin with the accents on the "Irv" and the "Ber".

The Hollywood Palladium was a great place, and my partners and I sat on the side of the stage for the seventeen years that Lawrence and the band appeared there for dinner and dancing, usually Friday and Saturday nights. In the earliest years, we'd have filmed the TV show all day Saturday, and then performed at the Palladium at night.

Sitting on the side of the stage was the way singers were called upon to perform in the big band days. We had a small space to execute our routines, but always did our best. Sometimes, Welk had guests. John Wayne came by, was very friendly, and I finally deduced he'd had too much to drink when he called Mr. Welk "Larry". He was always Lawrence or Mr. Welk.

The Armed Forces Radio Show was broadcast live with Lawrence's head writer, Ralph Portner, as host. Bob Crane of *Hogan's Heroes* would come by to play drums. Ronald Reagan, running for president, came by. I went up to the balcony, made the mistake of rustling the curtains while he spoke, and the Secret Service was on me in a flash.

Another funny incident I remember is when the Lennon Sisters were sitting stage left and were asked to sing. But before their song, a fan came up to Janet. "You're my favorite Lennon," he said, and placed his hand on her knee. Bam! Her leg reflex kicked him right in the face!

We had lots of audience regulars that came to the Palladium. There was a little dance couple we called "The Coles of Hollywood" who bounced across the floor with every tune. We also enjoyed watching the smooth but fast Balboa stylings (a form of swing dancing) of another couple, Johnnie and Madeleine Cristelli, who came every weekend.

Two of our popular singers, Bob Lido and Aladdin, were best friends. Two attractive, middle-aged ladies, who were also best friends, would regularly visit and stand in front of the bandstand. "Bachelor Bob" Lido ended up marrying one of those ladies, and her best friend married Aladdin in a double ceremony!

Lawrence even discovered some of his lady singers by inviting them up to sing and then putting them on the show as regulars. That's how popular singer Gail Farrell was discovered. Lawrence really didn't have regular auditions, and he never had contracts. A two-week notice was all that was needed for him to let you go or for you to leave on your own. He said it was a simple way to do things. And he always emphasized "keep it simple" with the band, singers, and even with our dances.

In keeping with the "simple" theme, Lawrence called Cissy and me into the office one day, and told us he wanted us to dance a simple, plain waltz, all dressed in white, around and around the ballroom set with no lifts just like they used to dance at the Aragon and Trianon Ballrooms when he played in Chicago. I said, "But Mr. Welk, our contemporaries won't think we're very good dancers, and will this be flashy enough to entertain our audience?" "Just try it and see," was his response. The dance floor was polished, chandeliers were in place, we were all dressed in white, and we floated smoothly across the floor to the song "Fascination". Lawrence knew his audience, and was always right about them. We got more response, and more fan mail, for our "beautiful ballroom" waltz than any other dance we did that season.

In 1982, Lawrence Welk did something he said he'd never do: play Las Vegas. He always felt that working in that town was not playing to his audience. Our engagement was at the MGM Grand and it was a salute to the movies. Elaine and I danced to *An American in Paris* with many changes in tempo. But once again Lawrence was right. His grandmas and grandpas don't stay up that late as our last show was at midnight and our audiences were just not there as they would have been at a more "normal" hour.

Appearing on the weekly TV show was just one aspect of my Welk career. I also spent many weeks each year traveling around the country making personal appearances. There are two particularly embarrassing incidents related to those trips that are forever etched in my mind.

The first embarrassment related to my appearance at Seal Beach Leisure World in Orange County, California, that my dancing partners and I played every year. This one time I was hurrying to make a band rehearsal. I rushed out of the house with my costume bag and music in hand and headed down the freeway. As I was getting dressed for the show, I realized I had forgotten my dress pants. So I told the gentleman who hired me and who was also the emcee. He was wearing a dinner jacket, so he loaned me his trousers. End of story? Nope. At the start of the performance, out comes the announcer and says, "Bobby forgot his pants, so my pants will be dancing for you this evening!"

Speaking of forgetting pants, Lawrence was so comfortable being our musical father, occasionally he would call us into his dressing room at the Hollywood Palladium just as he was putting on his pants. His 1930s garter belt for his socks looked awfully weird to us. Oops, should we be seeing him in his long john undies?

My second embarrassing incident happened in Ohio where the Copper Coin Ballet was honoring me for my dancing. The president of the company, a fan who'd become a friend, invited me to their tribute in my honor. To welcome me at the airport, he had arranged for a band to be lined up to play and banners were to be held up by the crowd of people gathered to meet the plane. The airline tickets were sent, but I had to change planes along the way. At the layover airport, my boarding area seats were all occupied, so I proceeded to sit at an adjacent gate's seat and became absorbed in a book. Well, I didn't hear my flight number called, and I missed my plane connection! Two hours later I arrived to but a few people, and half the banners had been torn down. This was the one time I felt like I really let my fans down. They forgave me, and their ultimate tribute was wonderful.

Sometimes even celebrities or celebrity relatives were big fans of the Welk show. One of them was movie star Randolph Scott's (a motion picture leading man whose career spanned the '20s through the early '60s) mother-in-law, Mrs. Stillman, who would invite Kristie and me to her apartment located in the Scott mansion in Holmby Hills, California. She would give us things like chocolates, pieces of jade, and vases. But what she gave us that meant the most were two sayings that we use to this day. "Life is a repair," meaning that things don't always go right and usually need fixing. The other made reference to children, especially teenage offspring. This one was our favorite: "Their problems are yours, their joys are their own!"

We got to meet the quiet, mild-mannered Mr. Scott himself. There he stood facing us, tall and handsome. My wife was star struck. He apparently was a dance fan because the first thing he said to me was, "How long does it take you to make up a dance routine?" We cherished our friendship with Mrs. Stillman. Sometimes, fans become personal friends.

Many of the Welk cast members also became lifelong friends. One group that will always hold a special place in my heart is the Lennon Sisters. I always loved working with them. They were truly the girls next door. And so very popular. They eventually got their own show on ABC with Jimmy Durante, and appeared on all the major variety shows, especially with Andy Williams. They've stayed good friends all these years. When they left, Lawrence hired Sandi and Sally, a popular singing duo, followed by singers Guy and Ralna and Tom Netherton. But during their time with the show, the audience loved the Lennons and the fan magazines were ravenous for them and the Welk stars.

Stories about the sisters and their big family of mom, dad, and eleven children were great fodder for such publications. My favorite off-the-wall headline read, "Janet Lennon—The Night I Became a Woman", referring to the evening of her sixteenth birthday party.

Lots of magazine coverage appeared when Lawrence Welk's son, Larry Welk Jr., married our girl singer, Tanya Falan. And when I married Kristie, we made headlines, too. My favorite was, "How Bobby Took His Bride Too Soon". As usual, the headline misrepresented the truth.

At a photo session before the big day, they had Kristie wear a pink lace dress. But when it was on the cover, the dress was shown as white and the shot was from the side with a slight poof in the tummy. We know what that implied. The issue sold like crazy. The magazine editor even bought us a sewing machine and gave us $1000 to take exclusive pictures of our wedding. Over the years, we've collected many more stories and covers, even featuring our kids.

The first of our four children, Becki, was born November 17, 1976, during filming of *The Lawrence Welk New Year's Show* that year. At the time of Becki's imminent birth, I was supposed to be rehearsing the Welk New Year's Show and I was scheduled to dance a Balboa with Cissy. Camera run-throughs came and went, no baby yet. But come dress rehearsal, I was nowhere to be found. I was at the hospital with Kristie. I did not want to miss that first birth! Who knew Kristie would have such a long labor. Yes, I missed the taping and Cissy danced alone, pretending she had a partner. Later that night, Becki made her debut. She was a beautiful baby. I was so proud to be in the delivery room. Lawrence let me show her picture on the next week's TV show. First time grandpa, Myron, flanked the photo with me.

On May 26, 1979, along comes Robert. Because he was the first male in the Floren line-up, he became Robert Floren Burgess. But I wasn't in the delivery room with Kristie this time. We couldn't schedule his arrival, so when the time came I was on tour with Myron on the East Coast. To this day, I have fans come up to me and say,

"I was in the audience at that theater-in-the-round the night you interrupted Myron's act to announce the birth of his first grandson, your son Robert."

Our second daughter, Wendi Ellen, was born on March 13, 1983, and she was adorable. By now, Kristie was known for her long labors, so the doctor went home for a rest. When the birth was suddenly imminent, the doctor was first stopped for speeding, then given a police escort to try to make it back to the hospital in time. He didn't make it. Guess who delivered Wendi? Yours truly and a little Jamaican nurse who exclaimed, "Oh, as a midwife, I've delivered many babies on the roads and in the fields of my country."

Finally, Brenton Christopher was born on November 22, 1986. Being the grand finale that he was, he was born on Kristie's November birthday, twelve days past his due date. I'd been hired for a Mouseketeer trip to Alaska thinking surely he'd be born by the time I needed to leave. Nine-pound, four-ounce Brenton preempted that date and the Mouseketeer show went on without me. I stayed home to be in the delivery room with Kristie. Now we have the perfect family, two boys and two girls. When we first married, we bought our dream house in the Hollywood Hills with a pool, a view of the valley, four bedrooms, and three baths. We live in it to this day.

From 1955 to 1971, *The Lawrence Welk Show* was a big ratings hit for ABC. Then they had a regime change and brought in a group of younger executives. We were cancelled. No ABC executives had the professional decency to inform Lawrence that his television show was cancelled. While he was on the golf links, one of his foursome mentioned, "Lawrence, I was sad to hear about you not being picked up by the network next season." Naturally, Mr. Welk was stunned! But Lawrence knew there was an audience for him and his music. So he started his own network to syndicate the show. And he more than doubled the stations he had with ABC.

Lawrence basically retired in 1982, but introduced reruns from Escondido, California, where he owned a mobile home park, until PBS (Public Broadcasting Service) picked up the show in 1987. Bob Allen was the gentleman who put it all together to get us on public television. He was the CEO of the Oklahoma PBS station in Oklahoma City. But it was his dad who suggested he pick up our weekly program for older folks to enjoy. Bob knew the Welk fans were not rich, but would make the show an appointment show, a favorite weekly show not to be missed, and support it by donating maybe $20.00 from their fixed incomes.

He was right. With the help of his right-hand man and our local director for wraparound intros, Bill Thrash, *The Lawrence Welk Show* has been seen on PBS since 1987 and is still running on many of the stations today. I am privileged to be asked to do pledge breaks all over the United States for PBS, and also have been honored to be the host of the show on alternating weeks with Mary Lou Metzger.

Our biggest PBS special, in March 2001, was called "Milestones and Memories", a reunion show. When the curtain went up on this special, filmed at the Welk Theater in Branson, Missouri, the entire living Lawrence Welk family, from 1955 to 1982, was there. Emceed by Janet Lennon, the show was very emotional, including for yours truly. The ovation was overwhelming, and you could feel the love come across the orchestra pit to the stage. It was one of my Welk highlights. The only thing that saddened me was that the maestro himself, who had passed away on May 17, 1992, wasn't there to share it with us.

Aired on PBS with pledge breaks between sections, it was thought that the show would bring in about $2 million. I am told it brought in $7 million! What a great success and testament to the popularity of Lawrence Welk.

During the show, Elaine and I got to dance to "Night and Day". The arrangement had three distinct parts, perfect for my three partners. I personally rehearsed each section with each partner. I called Barbara up, and she came to my house in the Hollywood Hills to my mirrored dance room to practice. I had her do the first part of the dance, a smooth twirling section with some small lifts.

Next came Cissy. She had semi-retired to Hawaii after her house was damaged in the 1994 Northridge, California, earthquake. She was selling real estate. We danced the middle part of the routine, a smooth fox trot. We hadn't danced together for 21 years, but it was like we'd never stopped dancing.

Then came Elaine. We were current, so the third part started with me carrying her in a grand jete lift across the stage, and we carried on from there to a standing ovation.

Other outstanding highlights, to me, were the reunion of five of the past Champagne ladies sitting on raised chairs sung to by Guy Hovis, then presented with roses. He sang his uplifting version of "Let the Eagle Soar", a patriotic song he later performed at George W.

Bush's second inauguration. Guy went on to be Senator Trent Lott's liaison to the U.S. Senate in Mississippi.

I appeared in all the PBS specials, fourteen of them. I missed number 15, a religious special. I guess they didn't like my suggestion to dance to a swing version of "When the Saints Go Marching In" or a waltz to the song "Going Home".

One of the great benefits of dancing on the show and traveling with the Stars of the Lawrence Welk Show for all those years was that I always stayed in good shape. Remember one of Lawrence's cardinal rules was to never gain weight. But I do love to eat, especially at the variety of restaurants I got to indulge at when I traveled all over the country for so many years. And my wife's a great cook!

So how did I stay in shape all those years for the TV show? Besides going to the gym and rehearsing two to four hours a day, my mother-in-law, Berdyne Floren, gave me a two-day diet where I could lose five pounds, and fit into my jumpsuit, quickly. For breakfast? A grapefruit squeezed into juice with three Equals, two eggs, and a piece of toast. Early dinner around 4pm consisted of a steak and sliced tomatoes. While watching TV before bed? A big glass of prune juice. It works!

I also seemed to need a little energy boost after dress rehearsal on TV taping day. Of course, we had done our dances with three camera run-throughs full out and then dress with an audience. One evening after dress rehearsal, a guy walked up and complimented me on my routine. He mentioned he was a wrestling coach, and that's when I asked, "Got any advice that you give to your wrestlers to pep them up?" "Sure do," he answered, and he told me he always gave them an orange and some honey. From then on, that was my menu between dress rehearsal and taping the show because I always tried to save my very best and most energetic performance for the actual TV show.

By now you're probably thinking I must have gotten paid tons of cash as a regular cast member on The Lawrence Welk Show. Some of today's TV stars, after all, earn upwards of $1 million per episode. But remember when I said Lawrence was of the frugal persuasion? That certainly came into play with salaries.

Lawrence Welk paid scale. For AFTRA members (that included all the on-air performers, including myself), it was $210.00 per show, which eventually went up to $285.00. In fact, sometimes after especially big applause for one of my dance numbers, he would say to the audience, "Don't give him such a big applause or he'll want a raise."

His other favorite in the same circumstance was, "Folks, don't give him such a big hand. He'll want to start his own band."

At the end of our filming in 1982, the band, because of the musicians union, was being paid a lot more than the cast members—$785.00 a show. But, I have no regrets. The series was a showcase for my talent. Lawrence actually told me when he first asked me to be a regular member of his organization, "If you catch on with my audience, you can do very well for yourself at fairs, club dates, and theater performances." And he was right; that's where I did very well. "Just give 10% to Sam Lutz (Lawrence's manager and mine as well)," he said, "and you'll be on your way." Few people know that Lawrence also put 15% away for us, if we stayed with him for 10 years or more, in a profit-sharing plan! I left the band with six figures just on that alone. Lawrence was always looking out for us and I could never replace the fun times I had with him, especially when he made us all laugh with his "Welkisms".

CHAPTER NINE

Welkisms

Lawrence Welk didn't speak English until he was 21 years old. He lived on a German dirt farm in Strasbourg, North Dakota, and that's why he had an accent. Occasionally, he had trouble with the English language and I called these bloopers "Welkisms".

When the boss would make a "Welkism", the band would laugh, and he would turn around, give them a serious look, and hit his behind multiple times with his baton. The following are some of my favorite "Welkisms":

- He was reading off his cue cards about World War One. "Ladies and Gentlemen, tonight we feature songs from World War Eye." (World War I)

- Addressing his band musicians: "Look like you're having fun, but don't have any."

- "Let's bring Barbara and Backy Bob!" meaning to say "Barbara and Bobby back," usually said at the Hollywood Palladium.

- "Here's our wunnerful dance team, Cissy and King!" (Am I a dancing horse?)

- Introducing a male singer, "Next, we're happy to have Alvin Ashby from right here in Evansville, Indiana. Alvin, come up here, and tell the folks your name and where you're from."

- "There are good days, and there are bad days, and this is one of them."

- We were in New Mexico at a Shrine Convention, and Lawrence had to introduce the Grand Potentate. Of course, we were in Indian country. "We're so honored to have with us tonight… uh…the chief Totem Pole!"

- Cissy had been dancing the polka with a German man from the audience. Lawrence suggested, "Cissy, if you're real lucky, this man will take you behind the bandstand, and give you a great big German sausage!"

- Anacani, another of our female tunesmiths, was about to sing while sitting on a stool downstage. Lawrence directed the guitarist, "Neil, go up and stand behind Anacani, and give her a good feel."

- "My records are selling like wild cakes." (hotcakes)

- "That's what really broke the camel's straw." (The straw that broke the camel's back)

- "Folks, stay after the show for the flashlights." (fireworks)

- "You know, I think she's one of those woman's ad-libbers." (women's libbers)

- "I wouldn't touch that lemon meringue pie with a ten foot pole."

- "That's my cup of dish." (tea)

- Introducing a guest performer: "His act may start out slow, but it tapers off."

- "I just had an idea that went right over my head."

- "Whenever you have a minute I'd like to see you right now."

- To a performer who apologized for being late and said he had no excuse: "That's no excuse."

- About a vocalist who auditioned: "She has a nice voice, but she looks a little bit too much like Eleanor Roosevelt."

- To the dress rehearsal audience about the use of a phony turkey on the set of a Thanksgiving show: "Don't worry, folks, this will be a real turkey when it gets on the air."

- "I just let it in one ear and out the top of my head."

- "You know, it's a long world."

- "Take a train." (Take the "A" train.)

- After a jet plane flew over and disrupted rehearsal: "You know, those jet planes make masonic booms."

- When an audience was not responding with generous applause: "I see we have a few sourpussies in the group tonight."

- When he found the Hollywood Palace stage to be too small to accommodate the whole band: "Fire four feet of the band."

- "I'm keeping perfect time. I'll get my barometer (metronome) and prove it."

- Then there was the time he accused a vocal group of being out of lip-sync when they were singing live.

- "Pee on your toes, boys." (Be on your toes, boys.)

- Inviting the Wisconsin Cheese Queen in the audience to come up on stage and dance: "Come up here and let us see you cut the cheese."

Lawrence Welk presents Bobby and Barbara.

In our red *Calcutta* outfits.

Um…Is Lawrence stealing my dance partner?

Mr. Welk presents us on *The Andy Williams Show* in 1963.

My favorite photo of my second partner, Cissy King, and myself.

Let's Charleston!

The latest moves for the 1970s.

Lawrence, Cissy, and I celebrate Welk's 15th year on TV.

A magazine cover with the Lennons.

Cissy and I step out with a polka.

Cissy accompanies me on the Rose Parade Float.

Jack Imel, Arthur Duncan, and I tap away as the "Three Steppers".

Peggy LeBaron shows me around Washington, D.C.

After Cissy leaves, Barbara comes back for 11 TV shows in 1979.

My third partner Elaine Niverson, in one of our first dances together.

One of my favorite photos with Elaine.

Elaine and I pose for the 1980s. Now she's Elaine Balden, having married.

On tour with Donald O'Connor, appearing on college campuses.

All three Welk dancing partners reunite with me for *Milestones and Memories* for PBS in Branson, Missouri, in the 1990s.

CHAPTER TEN

On the Road

On tour, a few people would come up, dance with Lawrence, and sit down. One was a guy named Bob Gerlack. He would come up and dance a wild stomping, hopping polka with Cissy and get a huge applause. Then Lawrence would say, "Thank you, Mr. Garlic." Another was a bespectacled woman named Genise Kurik. Lawrence would interview her. She would tell him her name then say, "I'm a school teacher." "Oh," Lawrence would say, "let me hold your glasses." They took dance position, and he would correct it. Then she would start dancing, and he would stop her and say, "Genise, right? In this dance team, I do the leading."

They would polka, and Lawrence would call me over and say, "Bobby, you dance with her, she's too wild for me." So we'd start, and then with hands overhead we'd spin very fast in place, and whoosh, her wig would go flying! Lawrence would cover his mouth, Genise would hide under the piano, and I would run to retrieve her wig and coax her back to the microphone. Lawrence would help her adjust her wig but make it crooked, which would get another laugh. Genise would walk off stage in tears. Then she'd hurry back and Lawrence would say, "She forgot her glasses." Genise would leave the stage. Yes, folks Genise was a "plant" in the audience and traveled with us…and so was Bob Gerlack.

This bit was always a smash until one night in Orlando, Florida. Whenever Genise came onstage, Lawrence would ask her where she was from, and she would find a Polish or German community nearby or a town with a funny name. That night, she said she was from KISSimee. Well, the town's name is pronounced KisSIMee. The audience knew right away she was a plant; and that was the only time we didn't get our huge laughs. To this day, people still come up to me and say, "I was in the audience when that girl lost her wig." For years, we were sworn to secrecy about our "plants", but finally Lawrence told the story in one of his books.

I've even adapted and used this audience bit in my own act for years. Of course, my partners and I had our own schtick. Usually when a man who is a lively sort comes up, while he is dancing with Elaine, for example, I will say, "See what happens when you take Geritol in the morning, and Sominex at night!" Or as the last man is finished with his polka and Elaine is walking him down to his seat, I'll say, "He looks like he's from the metallic age, gold in his teeth, silver in his hair, but definitely no lead in his britches!" Then we finish the act with a flashy step and overhead lift and bows.

Sometimes on tour I would be asked to do a local television show, and as I would get acquainted with the host, I would mention my love of water skiing. This paid off in a memorable early morning water ski in Montana, on the Missouri River, with leaves brilliant autumn colors, the river in mirror condition, and not another soul in sight. In Charleston, South Carolina, a morning television hostess treated me to a water ski around the Civil War era Fort Sumter, again beautiful glassy conditions, with dolphins leaping behind and on either side of me.

For seventeen years, we played at Harrah's Club in Lake Tahoe. Bill Harrah was very generous to everyone in the band. Lawrence got a beautiful home on Lake Tahoe with cook, housekeeper, and limo driver. Besides that, there'd also be a Cadillac for Lawrence's wife Fern to use when she would go to the club to drop silver dollars in the slots. Myron also got a house, Lake Haven, and a cook. This house also had a dock where I could tie up my "Bubble Machine" ski boat for waterskiing on Tahoe. But don't fall in, the water was about 52 degrees—wet suit necessary.

We did two shows a night for three weeks. Lawrence called it our "annual vacation". The first year or two, we even performed a third show at 2am. We packed 'em in and everyone always did their best routines competing for the most applause. We had a couple of super fans, senior citizens of course, who would come every year for every show. However, on occasion, we'd look down at them in their front row seats and catch them snoozing!

At Harrah's, Barbara and I made an especially big splash one year in the early '60s because we sang and danced rock 'n' roll. The song was "Lover Please", sung by me, and then we'd do the twist. Lawrence picked up on the enthusiastic response and called me into the office when we returned home. "Bobby, I want to make a record with you. The response to your singing in Tahoe was overwhelming."

The time, place, and original song were set, and I even had a rock band and back-up singers. The song I recorded was called "Poor Boy for Falling in Love", which was to be the flip side of a Welk single. I was proud of it, and looked forward to the release. Not to be. Our musical director, George Cates, had other plans. He jettisoned my record debut from side two, and put his original composition in its place. I was disappointed. Who knows? I could have been a rock star, but things happen for the best.

I did get to sing with Kathy Lennon when we filmed a show in Escondido. I was the elevator operator, she the passenger. Eventually my debut single was heard in public, at my daughter Becki's wedding reception, at her request.

Another big hit at Harrah's, and eventually on the television show, was a bit with Janet Lennon. Janet and I would come out polka dancing, but halfway through she would dance off to the wings and I would run after her. Bingo—a Janet look-alike dummy, dressed in an identical dress and wig, was waiting for me. Without skipping a beat, out we'd come, the dummy and me, one hand, one leg airplane style, and continue polka dancing as disco lights flashed. At the end, as dummy Janet flew over my head into the wings, out staggered the real Janet, wig askew, to applause from our stunned audience. What fun! Lawrence's idea again.

Every year when we played Harrah's, my Cal State Long Beach Sigma Pi Fraternity brothers would come to Tahoe for a long weekend to gamble, party, and attend a late Welk show. After a few drinks, they always had a great time. Lawrence would ask me, "When are those friends of yours from college going to come to see my show? They're such a wunnerful, wunnerful audience." When they did attend, Mr. Welk and the band knew it. My frat brothers whistled and shouted everyone's names which would give an extra boost to the performer, especially yours truly. A particular favorite of theirs was our tap dancer, Arthur Duncan. One overactive bro was even escorted out as he jumped on his chair for an especially enthusiastic response!

One of my very favorite dances I did with Cissy was "The Man I Love", by George Gershwin. It was one of Lawrence's epic big-band numbers. We performed it in Tahoe and then the following season danced it on the Welk TV show. Anyway, it was at a Tahoe performance of this dance that I remember one of my memorable "late Miss King" occurrences. At the announcement of the number, we're posed in the dark, center stage. Cissy is not there. I run out, but no Cissy. Zoom—out of the wings she runs and whispers, "I forgot my panties!" Uh oh! The music started and I panicked. With every spin I tried to hold her skirt down. Realize we're above the audience on that stage, so people are looking up! We finished the dance, ran off, and she said, "Well, I DID have on my tights." I was not happy.

In the '60s and '70s and into the '80s, theaters "in the round" were popular, especially on the East Coast. Westbury Music Fair was maybe the most prestigious out on Long Island in New York. Unfortunately, we didn't do great business there because they gave us Sinatra's hours, 7:30 and 10:30 p.m. shows. If people want to make money with Welk Stars, again the secret is bus tours and matinees (except for Tahoe for some reason). Our Geritol set likes to see our show, have a lunch or dinner afterwards, and be in bed when the sun goes down.

Some theaters-in-the-round were in tents, and of course, the humidity was not welcome on matinee days when you're doing a 30–45 minute dance act. A friend of Myron's first booked us at the theater-in-the-round in Cohasset, Massachusetts. Afterwards, we always signed autographs protected by a rope and guards. On a particularly hot afternoon, our great singer, Ralna, was standing next to me when an older gentleman walked up to her, asked for her autograph, and said, "This is the highlight of my life." With that, he keeled over and dropped dead of a heart attack right in front of us. Yikes! At least he died happy.

At one of these theaters-in-the-round, in Hyannis, Massachusetts, we were asked to fill in for Jim Nabors as the opening act for Robert Goulet at a moment's notice. We hopped the first plane out and arrived just in time. We rushed up on the stage for rehearsal, put our music down in front of the band, but noticed there was no drummer, piano player, or trumpet. What? We were missing maybe the three most important instruments in the band.

A band member said, "They're Mr. Goulet's personal players." So we went to Mr. Goulet's dressing room, met him, and explained our special circumstance. He was friendly, but said, "Talk to my manager." His reply? "No deal, you cannot use our guys." Fortunately, the booker knew the lady organist at the restaurant nearby who hurriedly came over to accommodate us and brought her own drum box, so we made it work.

Anacani, our ethnic Mexican American singer, became one of my very best friends on the Welk show. She called me "Sapo", which means frog in Spanish, because Kristie and I had a guest bathroom in our home with frog décor. I called her Consuelo, her real name, or occasionally Chiquita as in Chiquita banana.

She always had a perfect figure. She made her own dresses, so had to live up to her dress model. One day as we're all piling off for a quick lunch at McDonald's on a bus tour, I noticed she didn't accompany us. "Come on," I said. "No, Sapo, I have my apple and a granola bar." Discipline pays, she always looked beautiful.

Even today Anacani is very popular in Mexico and South America. When she was asked to do *Dancing with the Stars*, I thought she'd be perfect. She told them "no thank you". She didn't want to wear those peek-a-boo costumes and be thrown around and have to do splits.

I often got to meet celebrities while on tour with Lawrence Welk. In Peoria, Illinois, Shirley Temple was staying at our hotel. We were introduced, and I said, "Would you dance a little swing with me?" She smilingly obliged, and this adult Shirley was one of the best jitterbug dancers I'd ever danced with. She did the swivel, the sugar, and had that great swing feel. What a doll.

On our personal appearances, we loved dancing in front of some of the most famous big bands in the land. At a county fair in California, I'll always remember taking a mental picture of Count Basie, with his orchestra, staring down at us from a platform, smiling and playing "Calcutta". We waltzed and did our act while dancing to Wayne King, the Waltz King, who was not especially friendly. We jitterbugged in front of a drunken Sammy Kaye who was so soused that halfway through the act, his assistant took over.

Other famous names from the past that played our music for us were Freddie Martin at the Coconut Grove, the Buddy Rich big band, and the Glen Miller band directed by Tex Beneke at a fair in Missouri. This was an outdoor fair date and it was just dusk. Barbara and I were finishing our act with a lively Charleston when all of a sudden, a swarm of green-winged, airborne bugs landed on the wire of lights above our heads and then swarmed our dance floor. We slipped and slid across the buggy stage and for our ending Barbara fell into my arms with her legs up and BANG, both of us went down to thunderous applause. The audience loved the fact that we continued even though we had been slimed!

CHAPTER ELEVEN

All Over the Map

I've appeared in all fifty states multiple times. And I have a United States map with pins in each place I appeared, color coded with red for Barbara, silver for Cissy, and black for Elaine. I also have blue pins for *The Mickey Mouse Club*.

Back in the seventies, Cissy and I played many, many county fairs. One we did quite a few times was the Fresno District Fair. At this fair, they had wine tasting. At the end of the act during the polka segment, we invite audience members up to dance with us. Many obliged, but last to dance with me was a very serious lady who had tasted a little too much wine.

"Hey, be careful with me!" she barked. As a gag, I would dance the audience member around and then let go and do a polka twist which would usually get a laugh. Not this time! The lady, in slow motion, slipped and fell backwards, plop, and I ran to assist her by putting my arm around her shoulders and helping her off the stage. Do you know she sued me for $1500 because she said she hurt her back!!

After consulting with my attorney, he said "pay her off" because by the time we'd fly the two of us to court in Fresno with food, hotel, and attorney fees, it wasn't worth it to fight the outrageous demand. The fair had no insurance for dance acts with audience participation.

At another fair date, this one in Santa Rosa, California, during our polka audience participation bit, after dancing with a few participants, we noticed a bus pull up next to the stage. Out jumped twelve Downs Syndrome kids. All came up and we danced with each one. What a delightful group of youngsters. We loved it and the audience gave us a standing ovation.

At a fair in Pleasanton, California, we were signing autographs after the show on the outdoor stage. Some teenagers got behind me and pushed me into the audience. This must be how a rock star feels, as our senior citizens held me up over their heads and gently set me back on the stage.

At the Bakersfield Fair, our quick-change areas not only were outdoors and next to the stage, but they could be seen from the sides. Cissy lost a beautiful long orange dance skirt as a teen was heard to say, "This would make a great dress for the prom," grabbed her costume, and disappeared into the crowd before we could retrieve it.

At that time we were booked through a man named Bill Daly, a gentleman who had served in World War II and lost an arm. He had us play medium-sized venues where the Welk big band didn't play. It was usually Myron who led the band and did his act, me with my partner, Larry Hooper, Jack Imel, Dick Dale, Joe Feeney, JoAnn Castle, and occasionally the Lennon Sisters.

I remember I was missing two states where there were no pins on my map: Wyoming and Alaska. So I asked Bill to book us there. In Casper, Wyoming, we played in a large Holiday Inn banquet room. It sold out, and we were invited back the next year. In Alaska, the audiences were some of the best I'd ever performed for. They laughed the hardest at our jokes, gave our lifts the biggest hands, and were on their feet at the end with standing ovations. Well, I got my final pins in my last two states!

Touring in Milwaukee, I had one of my favorite "touristy" experiences. While the band checked into the hotel to eat and watch TV, I checked out the Schlitz Brewery. My guide was a friendly guy named Pat Nugent. As we got talking, I told him I was with the Welk band appearing at the auditorium, and he replied that he was a big fan of the Lennon Sisters, especially Janet. I told him we were leaving the hotel at 8a.m. the next morning, so if he came by, I'd introduce him to the Lennons.

Just as we were about to leave on the bus, bounding up the aisle is Pat! I introduce him to Janet and the girls, we exchange addresses for our Christmas card file, and that's it. Months later, I read that Pat Nugent is dating LBJ's daughter Luci "the Watusi" Johnson! Soon after that, I get an invitation to Luci and Pat's wedding in Washington, D.C. Barbara and I attend, meet the President and Lady Bird, Lynda Bird, and her then current beau, actor George Hamilton, and are floored when the newlyweds ask Bobby and Barbara to polka right in the White House! I still have a piece of their wedding cake in a satin box.

Years later, our Stars of the Lawrence Welk Show were being showcased in Austin, Texas. I give Pat and Luci a call. He's now running the family radio stations, and she is the mother of four. They invite us over after seeing our show, give us some food and drink, and show us their coveted wedding gifts from heads of state across the world. All of this because I went touring at the Schlitz brewery.

One time being the tourist in the group got me into trouble. On tour in Memphis, the bus was taking the band to the hotel. I was sitting close to the bus driver, so I asked him, "Isn't this the city that's the home of Elvis Presley?" He answered that it was. Elvis lived in Graceland which was just a few blocks away. "Great," I said, "maybe you could drive by."

Well, it wasn't a few blocks away, but several miles away. Aladdin, our violinist, was sitting across from me and asked, "Hey, what's taking so long? The band and I are tired and want to go to the hotel." The driver replied, "Bobby wanted to go by Elvis' house." "What!!" screeched Aladdin. I felt that if the band had rotten tomatoes, they would have all thrown them at me. We drove by Elvis' house, then to the hotel. I got ribbed the rest of my days by the band whenever the bus took a little longer to get to its destination. "Bobby, did you tell the bus driver to go by Elvis' house!!"

In 1982, the Welk TV series ended its network TV run. The man who managed the Welk performers on the show and off, Sam Lutz, retired. We performers became a ship without a rudder, having no representation. Ralna and I took it upon ourselves to find somebody to pick up the reins. Then it struck me! Liberace had since passed away, and I thought if I could find who managed him, we might have the perfect fit because Liberace's audience and the Welk audience were the same.

We tracked down Seymour Heller and contacted him. He enthusiastically replied that he would love to represent us. So from the 1980s on, Seymour got us state fairs, theaters-in-the-round, and club dates. This little man and his valise, usually filled with money, became our friend and traveled with us on most of our dates.

In 1994, our opportunity for even more live appearances came about when Larry Welk Jr. opened The Lawrence Welk Champagne Theatre starring the Lennon sisters, the Lennon Brothers, and many of us in the Welk family, including myself, in Branson, Missouri. At that time Branson was the Midwest capital of entertainment with many stars building their own theaters and appearing at them throughout the year. With the Welk Theater thriving, the Lennon Sisters actually moved their whole families to Branson and made it their home base. Elaine and I were fortunate to dance on that stage for seven years, along with JoAnn Castle and my good friend Ken Delo as emcee.

Everybody was so friendly in Branson. I was talking to a security guard backstage, and he was telling me he used to be a policeman on Lovers Lane. One night, he was walking his beat and he noticed three cars parked there. So he walked up to the first one, knocked on the window, and there was a couple smooching in the back seat. He said, "What're you doin' in there?" And they replied, "Just doin' the slow fox trot." He said, "Better get a move on, this is a dangerous area."

He approached the second car, knocked on the window, and there was a couple kissing and hugging in the back seat. Again he said, "What's happening in there?" and they replied, "Just doin' the cha-cha-cha." And he said, "You'll have to leave NOW!"

Then he went to the third car. The windows were all fogged up, and there was a couple necking in the front seat. As before, he knocked on the window and the girl sat up. The cop said, "I suppose you're doing the Bossa Nova." "Nope," she replied, "I'm doing the boss a favor." I love those stories about dancing! I tell it in my act. That's about as blue as I get.

Sometimes on tour we'd come across musical obstacles. In Iowa, at a county fair, they had us dancing on a slab of raised concrete with just a lady organist on the side who could barely read music. In Massachusetts, we were appearing at the fairground amusement area, competing with the ferris wheel and roller coaster noises. But that wasn't the worst! An inept polka band was our accompaniment. But this group, and especially the accordionist leader, skipped bars such that he, nor we, ever knew where we were in the routine. As a solo act, it wouldn't have been so bad, but to coordinate steps and lifts was, to say the least, a challenge. But the bandleader was the nicest guy, and he invited us to his house afterwards for a big meal and a swim in his pool.

Another time, a friendly fan at a county fair appearance invited us over between our first and second shows for a big spaghetti dinner. Unfortunately, Cissy didn't have the brakes on, consumed large quantities of food, and that night, I practically needed a crane to get her up to the lifts!

We played the Corn Palace in Mitchell, South Dakota, for many years with Lawrence and the Welk band, and after Lawrence passed away we continued to play it with Myron and the Welk Stars. We were inevitably invited to a pheasant dinner, buckshot and all, but much appreciated, of course. The walls outside the Corn Palace were decorated with scenes of South Dakota all made out of corn and husks.

Occasionally, our band guys would meet an attractive young lady at our gigs. One year at the Corn Palace, Buddy Merrill, our shy guitarist, met a cute teenager and had a brief romance with her. Since we were there with our Stars of the Lawrence Welk Show, we'd chartered a plane to take us to the next date. We were all on the plane, but no Buddy. Zoom! His rented car came barreling up and he jumped out and up the stairs just as we noticed a farmer with a shotgun, teenage daughter beside him, speeding up to the plane in his pick-up. Up went the stairs, and we were off, averting a "farmer's daughter and irate father' scenario!

Kenny Trimble, nicknamed KT, one of our trombonists, always sat in the shotgun seat in the front of our touring buses. Being good friends, but putting him on and calling him Cowboy, KT would yell "Yee Haw" when our country singer Clay Hart would board. Until one stop. Clay boarded first and sat in KT's seat. He had a cream pie in hand, and as we all anticipated, on gets Kenny, and splat! A pie in the face to laughter and applause.

Larry Hooper, the man with the deep voice, was a band piano player when Lawrence discovered he could sing. Larry was given a lot of character parts on the show because of his sense of humor. And here's my Hoopie story. He had worked in vaudeville with a dance act named Hibbert and Leroy. Now, MR. Hibbert had an unrepaired cleft palate, and at the end of his beautiful dance act, he would say, "I thank you, and MISS Hibbert thanks you."

Larry delighted in telling us this story. And then he started calling Barbara and me Leroy and Miss Hibbert. He'd also been at a banquet where Lawrence Welk had accidentally belched, loud enough to be heard at the far end of the table. So now he would walk past Barbara and me with an "Ah," with that low voice of his simulating a burp. I was Leroy to Hoopie ever after.

On a trip to Washington, D.C., word was sent backstage to see if anyone would like to see the sights of the capitol. Dick Dale said, "Talk to Bobby. He's the tourist." So an older, well-dressed lady came backstage and introduced herself as Peggy LeBaron. She was a big fan, had been a Ziegfeld Follies dancer, and was widowed by the death of her husband, the first United States Atomic Energy Commission head. "May I pick you up tomorrow morning? Just look for the black limo."

Wow, what an adventure! Peggy knew everybody, and she was invited to all the best D.C. parties. Later I learned she was always requested to do the Charleston at these gatherings. She got me a private tour of the White House and lunch in the Senate dining room where John Glenn and Robert Byrd came over to say "hi" to Peggy and introduce themselves to me. She took me behind the scenes at the Supreme Court, then to Roger Stevens' office, the president of the Kennedy Center. And the next year when the Welk band played the Armory again, she invited Kristie to join us. This time, we also toured George Washington's home, Mount Vernon. Another example of how being the "tourist" in the band really paid off.

When touring with Elaine playing state and county fairs, club dates, theaters-in-the-round, and one-night appearances, we sometimes had some real unusual things happen. The first time we appeared together was in Elaine's hometown of Dallas, Texas. She was really kicking up her heels that night. In fact, she kicked her leg so high, her shoe ended up in a lady's lap in the front row.

Another time, we were at a big state fair with the band. We were all dressed in white, doing the Charleston. I kicked up one foot, the other foot slipped out from under me, and we ended up doing The Black Bottom!

I got a chance to tap dance with our tap dancer extraordinaire, Arthur Duncan and Jack Imel on tour with the big band. We were in Waterloo, Iowa, at the Cattle Congress in front of 12,000 people. Years earlier, when Lawrence had appeared at the Chicago Theater in Chicago, he saw the famous, flashy tap dancing act, The Step Brothers. Their specialty was each of them trying to outdo the next with applause-rousing combinations of steps and jumps at the end of the act. Lawrence thought if he'd put the three of us together, we could do the same thing. He dubbed us The Three Steppers. Once, I was doing my grasshopper bounce step that ends in the splits and ripped my pants right up the back.

We played many state and county fairs, and sometimes the floors were not the cleanest. One fair had the worst floor we'd ever danced on. It was out amongst the pigs and chickens. It was made of warped plywood and had holes in it that we had to dodge while dancing. Elaine and I were doing the swing and preparing for one of our big steps. So I kicked over her head, slid her through my legs, and... she had splinters for about two weeks. (I didn't pull them out, her husband did.)

In our act, I tell the audience that I had a ball being one of Walt Disney's original Mouseketeers. Then I have them sing the alma mater with me, "M-I-C-K-E-Y, M-O-U-S-E." Walt Disney would have been proud. Then I go into the audience, mouse ears in hand, and say, "Here's a lady who's really been enjoying our show." I ask for her name and say, "I'd like to make you an honorary Mouseketeer." The music starts and I do the whole routine. "Step right up, here's your ears, you're an honorary...Mouseketeer." As I place the autographed ears on her head, I say, "Welcome to the club." It was always a fun piece of nostalgia for me. I don't know what happened to all those ears I gave away. Hopefully, grandchildren have enjoyed playing with them.

CHAPTER TWELVE

Cotillion Master

My original dance teacher, Mrs. Call, gave me a valuable saying, "If you fail to prepare, prepare to fail." That was in 1988 when she became my first cotillion business partner. I was no longer a part of a weekly television series, so I was open to a new venture. She provided the perfect opportunity.

Out of the blue, Mrs. Call contacted me to assist her in teaching cotillion ballroom dancing after her husband, Derrall, passed away. At first, I was unsure if I wanted to be a Cotillion Master. After all, I had performed all my life. But when I got into it, I realized it was very creative. I loved finding just the right music for each dance. Thank goodness for all those great Lawrence Welk CDs.

We proceeded to work together for two years at the Lakewood Country Club in Lakewood, California. Then, Betty Outen and Linda Rowe, two women whose children were attending a Yacht Club Cotillion nearby, became disgruntled with their instructor, so they created a Call's Cotillion at the Long Beach Golden Sails Hotel Crystal Ballroom. Soon after, Chloe married and relocated to St. George, Utah. She often told me, "I think you're the only one who can continue our cotillion," and she virtually handed it over to me when she left. It was my lucky day. It became the Burgess Cotillion.

Meantime, Chloe's sister, Florence Wiseman, knew all about etiquette and manners having worked Chloe's cotillions all those years. Florence became my manners lady. She was a real character, very funny, yet sincere and loving, and extremely popular with the kids and parents.

Two friends, Rob and Carol Thomas, who had taken second place in the Lawrence Welk "Calcutta" contest that Barbara Boylan and I had won so long ago, became my senior teachers. And Carol Thomas is my manners lady since Mrs. Wiseman passed away. Eventually, all four of my children would become Burgess Cotillion teachers, along with Florence's daughter, Camarie DeWeese. It's always been a family affair.

Next, an enthusiastic chairwoman, Monica Brady, became my coordinator and stayed with the program for eighteen years. We also created a junior teacher program for outstanding cotillion students who graduated out of the classes, but who wanted to remain connected to cotillion as teacher aides.

Cotillion is a party! We teach ballroom dancing, manners, and etiquette, and the kids make new friends, all in a fun, yet structured environment. We just have three rules: no talking when someone is on the microphone; no gum chewing; and the Golden Rule of Cotillion, never refuse to dance. We don't want hurt feelings from rejection, plus we change partners every thirty seconds or so.

We had one unfortunate situation regarding gum chewing which proved the wisdom of that particular rule quite clearly. One evening, a beautiful girl with long blond hair was dancing near a sliding glass door next to the patio. She was chewing gum with her mouth open. Chomp, chomp, chomp. Well, along came a sudden breeze that blew her hair into her mouth. We had to take her into the lobby and cut off some of her hair to get the gum out! Obviously, she didn't chew gum again at cotillion after that. Neither did anyone else.

Our ballroom dances each season are the waltz, foxtrot, and swing. As for the Latin dances, we alternate each year between samba, cha-cha, and merengue one year, and salsa, tango, and rhumba the next. Our swing dance style changes as well. One year it's West Coast triple time swing, the slower, in-the-groove, swing, and the next year it's East Coast single time swing, or jitterbug.

And where will students ever use these dances? At country clubs, weddings, bar mitzvahs, or on cruises. If nothing else, we want our students to be able to waltz at their own weddings!

We also hope they will remember the manners we teach them for the rest of their lives, both socially and for business. We explain the tenets for good manners in a hands-on way. We bring in a table, and present table manners. We teach them how to start and hold a conversation with someone new by using the H.E.L.P. strategy. "H" is for asking about their hobbies; "E" for asking what they like to do for entertainment; "L" is for what are their particular likes; and "P" is for their future plans.

We also instruct students how to introduce people by using "The Four Gs." Those whose titles begin with "G"—Girls, Grandparents, Grown-ups, Guest of Honor—are said first in order of introduction.

We relate computer and telephone manners, how to sit properly, how to take refreshments, and how to go through a reception line.

Through cotillion, we hope to instill our students with self-confidence and respect for themselves, each other, and others. We begin the party by saying, "If you help someone else to have a good time, you'll have a good time yourself." We finish each season with a waltz contest. Winners are awarded trophies and prizes. At this dance, we also invite parents to enjoy mother-son and father-daughter dances with their children.

I've always tried to be as current as possible with the music that I use at cotillion. It's always danceable but without any offensive language. Since I had done all my own choreography on the Welk show all those years, I took pride in using all my own steps, but also in finding new dances, new steps, and new social mixer specialty dances that change partners in formation. I found I loved teaching cotillions!

Then in the cotillion season of 1991-1992, two ladies from Palos Verdes (an affluent LA coastal city in the hills) were looking for someone to guide their cotillions. Mitzi Cress and Lori Beck visited Burgess Cotillion and exclaimed, "Wow! Your kids can really dance, and they're having fun, too." They then invited me and my staff to come to Palos Verdes and teach at three middle schools and also guide their high school group, called the Assembly.

The Assembly consists of over 220 ninth to twelfth grade high school students. We teach them to dance, and emphasize manners. Besides Assembly membership, they are required to perform a minimum of twenty hours of volunteer service to the community. For the high school seniors, we have an annual Presentation Ball at the Biltmore Hotel in downtown Los Angeles where we present boys as well as girls. I choreograph a Viennese waltz in formation for mothers and sons, and one for fathers and daughters. The girls appear in full white ball gowns and the boys in black tails. It is always a truly memorable night for all.

In total, I own and preside over five cotillions. Having such an enjoyable work life gives me the privilege of teaching over 1800 young people each year and employing my family, my friends, and the Call's relatives. The cotillions also allow me to work with wonderful patronesses and chairwomen who have volunteered their time and efforts to make these endeavors the successes they are today.

While my cotillions are mostly fun for everyone involved, we've also had some "wild" things happen. Hidden whoopee cushions sat on at quiet moments during teaching, stink bombs set off at inopportune moments, and the most memorable, streakers.

The first occurrence of streaking happened at one of the Palos Verdes Middle School cotillions. As our manners lady was speaking, the curtain behind her opened suddenly, and three naked boys ran across the stage. The next time, a group of eight barged in, chanted in a center circle, and ran out.

The third time was really memorable. As our eighth grade cotillion reception line was concluding, I heard a yell across the hall near the refreshment table. There stood three teenage boys with head bandanas, shades, and flannel shirts wrapped around their waists, and that's all. One ran out the side door, another ran out the back door, and the third ran toward me headed for the door behind. I thought, if I deck this guy, I'll get sued. So instead, I left a big handprint on his back as he whizzed by me. A week later, these same teenagers streaked the middle school lunch area. Two coaches on duty tackled and captured them and saw to it they were expelled for their hijinks.

Another time, while I was teaching my cotillion at the Petroleum Club in Long Beach, I noticed an older man staring at me, and then motioning me over. Come to find out he was inebriated, nearly ready to fall off his stool at the bar. But then the surprise! "Hey, you're that Mouseketeer guy, Bobby!" he slurred. "Tell me all about "Spin and Marty"!" He turned out to be a big, big *Mickey Mouse Club* fan and asked me about all the roll-call kids. No matter where I go or how old I get, I still wear those ears and I'm proud of it.

CHAPTER THIRTEEN

Around the World

Traveling, for vacation fun, is a big part of my family life. Kristie and I travel as a couple or with a group, and love it when the whole family can join us. In fact, I have a world map in my home covered with pins placed in every location we've ever visited. Thankfully, I was able to earn a living that has allowed us to travel near and far.

Our top family vacation was to Kenya, where we saw more wild animals than you could imagine. Brent, my youngest son, and I went on the best snorkeling adventure of our lives when we visited Zanzibar, off the coast of Tanzania, as an African add-on. Masai warriors liked Brent. He was about their age and height. As a special gesture they thought he'd like to partake in one of their special beverages and asked, "Do you like blood?"

We also took the whole family to Egypt, a destination not to be missed. Cancun, Acapulco, and Cabo San Lucas in Mexico were memorable. A top favorite was Costa Rica. We all loved Tahiti, and we always have a great time in Hawaii. We took the train across Canada and stayed at the famous chateau hotels, especially enjoying Lake Louise and the Calgary Stampede.

Kristie and I adventured to India as I wanted to see the Taj Mahal and the Ganges. Neither of us are big fans of Indian food. After a three-week tour, the hotel at our last stop had a nice patio restaurant that boasted hamburgers, milkshakes, and French fries on the menu. I missed American food so much, I ordered them instantly. Delicious. But wait. The aftermath. That night, I developed chills, fever, and eliminations via mouth and you-know-where. The waiter explained that they do not eat beef because the cow is sacred. I had eaten a goat burger! The positive ending? I lost ten pounds.

Another top destination was exotic Bali. We also cruised the Greek Isles from Athens to Istanbul on the Windstar sailing ship. I have a bucket list and cross out names of countries we visit in addition to "pinning" them on my map. When we sailed down the Amazon on a cruise ship, we started in Manaus. A friend said that we missed going up one of the small tributaries and seeing local peoples and animals. So I had to add Iquitos in Peru and the upper Amazon to my list. We went to Antarctica as Kristie's choice with an add-on to Easter Island, my choice, and have just returned from Paris and environs, our third visit there. A vacation to the British Isles was memorable, and Eastern Europe and Russia were fascinating. We also love Venice.

A number of years ago, Mouseketeer Sherry Alberoni invited Kristie, Brent, and me to come to her daughter's wedding in Rome. Sherry and her husband, Dr. Richard Van Meter, are very active in the Catholic Church. In fact, for many years he served as a Medical Director that takes seriously ill folks to the healing waters of Lourdes.

Their daughter Kelly was to be married in Rome because it was where her fiancée's many family members called home, although Andrea, the groom to be, and his parents had relocated to southern California many years prior. In order that all the other members of the family still in Italy could attend, the wedding was held at the Vatican! That's right, in the Chapel of the Choirs. Following was an elaborate reception at a chateau on a hill south of Vatican City overlooking Rome where presidents, kings, and queens are entertained. Mouseketeer Cheryl Holdridge, who also attended the festivities, treated us to dinner on the night following the wedding, at the city's best restaurant atop the Spanish Steps overlooking Rome.

In the days prior to the ceremony, Sherry and Rich had arranged for Kristie and I along with a few of their family members to tour the catacombs beneath the Vatican to see St. Peter's tomb and bones. We also had a private tour of the Sistine Chapel.

After the wedding festivities, Brent, Kristie, and I extended our trip and took a Baltic cruise from Stockholm to Copenhagen. The highlight was the Hermitage Museum in St. Petersburg.

We've also experienced the Panama Canal and visited many Caribbean islands. We cruised around the Galapagos Islands off of Ecuador to see the giant tortoises, blue-footed boobies, seals, and iguanas. We've explored South America and toured Machu Picchu, and danced the tango in Buenos Aires and the samba in Brazil. We took a tour to China and also visited Angkor Wat in Cambodia, stepping inside many temples formerly off limits because of the Khmer Rouge holocaust. We recently cruised down the Danube from Nuremberg to

Budapest to partake of the famous Christmas markets. We enjoyed lots of mulled wine and sausages. We bought a polka-dancing cuckoo clock among other things, and because it was the dead of winter, we also nearly froze. But, so memorable.

Brent and I enjoyed a father-and-son rafting adventure down the Colorado River in the Grand Canyon. As a family, we have made numerous trips to Las Vegas, one of our favorite destinations for the great shows. On our way to a Floren family reunion in Sioux Falls, South Dakota, we stopped at Yellowstone, saw Mr. Rushmore, and the Badlands. Also on this trip, we visited Strasburg, North Dakota, Lawrence Welk's hometown, and toured his family farm and homestead escorted by his nieces.

What else is on that bucket list? The Holy Land and Petra, the Mardi Gras, and the Land of the Midnight Sun to see the Northern Lights. We're hooked on travel! And because we love to shop everywhere we go, we'll probably have to move out of our home soon as eleven china cabinets are stuffed with our souvenirs, or "tchotchkes", as my wife calls them.

When we cruised Alaska, the highlight was a helicopter ride with beautiful, majestic music playing in our earphones as we soared over the glaciers. We landed and embarked on a dog sled ride that was the highlight of that trip.

In England, we rented a car and drove clear down south to Land's End, and then up to northern England. It was here that adventurous Bobby with Kristie, in our rental car, veered off the paved country road onto a dirt road after seeing a sign that pointed toward a bed and breakfast in that direction. The detour earned me the nickname "Clark", as in Clark Griswold of the *Vacation* movies.

I am ever the eternal, smiling optimist who never shies away from any would-be adventure, even when I should listen to the rational, logical people around me. As we drove down this unpaved road, it got smaller and smaller until my wife quietly said, "Maybe this isn't the way to the bed and breakfast."

"Oh, sure it is, and it's going to be a great one at the end of this little road!" I countered. Well, we kept driving, the road got so small that it was merely the width of my car; and when a huge boulder suddenly appeared in front of me, I knew Kristie had been right. I couldn't back up, the tires just spun. What to do? We hear clip clop, clip clop. We're in a narrow gully. We look up and see a local farm girl riding her horse. "Is this the way to the bed and breakfast?" I call from below. "No, this is the bridle path," she replies. Well, we were stuck. Lucky for us, her dad was a local farmer. She went to get him. When he returned, he tied a rope to our bumper and pulled us out with his tractor. I bet he's told the story of the crazy Americans who drove down the horse path a time or two since.

In China, early one morning, we heard music from our hotel coming from behind the old city walls. We got up and made our way to the source. On the way, we passed a large group of people practicing Tai Chi. Other groups gathered to exercise together as well. Finally, we found the music. There, in a circular area, were about two hundred people ballroom dancing! So, we joined in, and before you know it, we were tapped on our shoulders and danced along with the locals. They were excellent dancers.

Sometimes, the most memorable things on travels are the surprises that happen, activities that aren't even planned. I climbed the Great Wall on that same trip, eight towers' worth, even though I'd had a hip replacement just three months earlier. Arthritis had set in after an automobile accident ten years previous. I let the doctor know about my Great Wall hike, and my story made the cover of his newsletter.

In Norway, we hit a little town at the head of the Stavanger Fjord on Norwegian Independence Day, May 17. Our bus tour just happened to be there during this happy occasion. During the day, we saw flags and parades of people in traditional costume. In the evening, there was folk dancing and feasting in the basement hall of our hotel. We joined the locals in a lively country waltz. That tour also took us to Oslo and the Vigeland Sculpture Park with myriad beautiful sculpted human bodies. We also visited Hans Christian Andersen's Denmark and Keukenhof Gardens in Holland with thousands of tulips and hyacinths in full bloom.

We love going to Turkey. We had the greatest shopping experience at the Grand Bazaar in Istanbul. We visited gorgeous mosques and yachted on the Bosphorus. We ventured under the city where there is a huge cistern built by the Romans. We talked our tour group into two things: going to see the whirling Dervishes and having a Turkish bath. The bath was interesting. They scrubbed you so hard, it felt like your skin would fall off. Then they demanded a tip!

Also on this same trip, our travel agent had arranged for us to tour Ephesus, an ancient Greek city in ruins. At night she arranged a private dinner served in front of the library in Ephesus. It was tended by a swarm of butlers and cats! After dinner, we all stood up, and to help us digest, I taught our group the Virginia Reel square dance. What a location.

We took our family on a cruise up the Mississippi River where Kristie said she had the best lobster of her life. We stopped at plantations and visited Natchez. In Vicksburg, we attended a formal Ball where we felt like we were back in the pre-Civil War days. In Baton Rouge, we took an excursion out in the Bayou to an old wooden cabin, tasted alligator, and learned a Cajun dance to Zydeco music. It came in handy for my cotillion Mardi Gras-themed dance.

A week after we got home, my agent called and asked, "How would you and Elaine like to perform on the *Mississippi Queen* steamboat?" Of course I said yes, and we performed on a sister ship, the *American Queen*, the following year. But it was worth the $10,000 I paid to take the whole family for fun the very first time.

We loved Rio de Janeiro with all its great music and samba shows. We also loved Buenos Aires with its underground tango dance shows where the plentiful "hostesses" pushed drinks on the clientele. On Rio's Ipanema Beach, we went to a fine restaurant. I just wanted a salad. Kristie reminded me that we weren't supposed to eat raw vegetables. But I didn't listen because it was the best restaurant in town! That salad was a big mistake. After dinner, as Kristie and I walked across the beautiful sandy beach, the moon was full, and it should have been a romantic moment. Then it hit.

Heading back to the street, I had this horrid cramp, and then I started running. I only got halfway back until I couldn't wait. I had to dig a hole in the sand, and make a deposit right there. It was pitch dark that night, except for the occasional voodoo candles lit in the sand. I hope no one saw me! The same thing happened at the Incan ruins in Machu Picchu, Peru. This time, when I had an attack, I made it behind a bush, only to look up and see a German tourist taking my picture!

CHAPTER FOURTEEN

The Best of Times

A few years ago, my wife Kristie and I were invited to the opening of the Walt Disney Family Museum in San Francisco. Diane Disney Miller, Walt's daughter, created this awesome institution that is dedicated to her father, his innovations, and his genius.

Throughout, Walt's voice illustrates exhibits, many of them interactive. I was so pleased to find that Diane included a lovely tribute to the Mouseketeers. I understand that she made *The Mickey Mouse Club* gallery a special project. Apparently, she and her sister, Sharon Disney Lund, were big Mouse Club fans.

At the opening reception of the Museum, Kristie and I were seated at a table with a few of Walt's granddaughters. They made me feel very special when they said that when they'd go over to their grandma Lillian's house on Saturdays, she'd have the Welk Show on, and proudly proclaim, "That's Bobby, our original Mouseketeer." Of course, Mr. Disney had to have been there occasionally to see me dance, too.

He would have loved our "Salute to Disney" on the Welk show. It had great Disney music, and I think he would have enjoyed my "Mickey Mouse Mambo" number with our principals in name shirts and ears, doing roll-call, singing, and playing instruments, with Cissy and me dancing. Recently, Sam Gennawey, my Disney-loving brother-in-law and author of several Disney books, said he had spoken to Diane Disney Miller, and she told him that Bobby was always her favorite Mouseketeer. A real compliment!

Diane was an especially lovely lady. I did an interview for a video about her dad, and she sent me a case of wine from The Silverado Winery that she owned with her husband, Ron Miller. We continued to send Christmas cards back and forth for years. Sadly, Diane passed away in November 2013 from injuries sustained in a fall. But, with the creation of the Walt Disney Family Museum, she established a great legacy to her father and to his descendants to be enjoyed by millions in the decades to come.

Most of us Mouseketeers have a great fondness for our Disney association even to this day. As our Alma Mater song said, "Through the years, we'll all be friends", and it's true. Many of us have stayed very close even through the next generation of our families. For example, my son Robert and Mouseketeer Tommy Cole's son Casey are best friends.

We mice also see each other at weddings, unfortunately sometimes at funerals, and special Disney events like Disneyana conventions and collector's shows. Plus, in the '80s and '90s Mouseketeer Sherry and I toured, along with our long-time Disney publicist and good friend, Lorraine Santoli, throughout the United States and points beyond to spread the Disney message (whatever the company wanted us to promote at the time).

We had so many fun adventures on those trips, and Disney was footing the bill for our first-class airfare and five-star hotels. Our promotional agendas were set in advance in each city that we visited, and all we had to do was talk about *The Mickey Mouse Club* and Disney's latest projects that the Disneyland PR folks or Disney corporate executives wanted promoted. For "Mickey's 60th", in 1988, we visited twenty-five cities nationwide, each day doing TV, radio, and print interviews. And after each long day of working, we'd always head out for a great dinner afterwards, and if we were up to it, visit some of the city's hotspots.

We always had a lot of fun with radio interviews, although we never knew when an unexpected question would pop up. One of the most memorable was in Texas. This swingin' host, who was proud to boast he was "live", asked us the usual questions, then said, "Do you Mouseketeers ho each other?" I think I said, "as in hey there, hi there, ho there?" and Sherry followed up with "like ho ho ho good times?" That was not what he meant. We quickly concluded that interview.

In Detroit, we appeared with the mayor at a TV press conference and received, along with Mickey Mouse who was with us on this particular trip, the keys to the city. Unfortunately, the mayor was soused and there was a pack of news cameras covering the event and picking up every word and gesture.

In the midst of the shaky presentation, the Mayor suddenly got off the "Disney" track and started to talk about Detroit issues that were relevant at the time, particularly their serious drug problems. Oh no…there were Sherry, me, and Mickey Mouse cuddled up to the inebriated mayor on a rant about drugs! Lorraine, our publicist, was in the back of the room motioning for us to move out of the shot. For some reason, we thought she was indicating that we should move closer to the mayor, so we did. She then started wildly waving at us, and I guess we finally got the message and moved off the stage.

At Bloomingdale's in New York, also as part of Mickey's 60th, we did a meet-and-greet and our autograph line was huge. Michael Eisner, then CEO of Disney, and his wife, Jane, were there. Michael said, "Wow, look at the huge response to the original Mouseketeers," and the concept for a *New Mickey Mouse Club* was born.

In fact, when plans for the *New Mickey Mouse Club* were unveiled, the executives called a few of us originals in for a conference at the studio to tell us about their ideas for the new show. As they continued talking, I interrupted, saying, "You have some good ideas, but are you going to have the new Mouseketeers singing 'Old McDonald Had a Farm' and the "Green Grass Grows All Around?'" They smiled and said no, they were going to rap the "Mickey Mouse March". Also, no name shirts or ears. "But what about Mickey?" I asked. No, they weren't having the "rubber mouse". I knew it was going to be a different show!

The first-year kids were talented. No big names emerged, although a good rock group called The Party was created. All were dismissed after one year, and a whole new group replaced them. I was even sent to auditions accompanying Matt, the first-year casting director. Out of the second group came Brittany Spears, Ryan Gosling, Christina Aguilera, Kerry Russell, and Justin Timberlake, who happens to be my neighbor in the Hollywood Hills.

In the *New Mickey Mouse Club's* first year on the air, a group of us originals were sent to Walt Disney Studios in Florida (part of the Walt Disney World property) where the new club was filming a special for their first anniversary. We did our '50s medley of singing and dancing, and they did their current '80s schtick. Then, we switched. Their great choreographer gave us all the current moves, and the new Mouseketeers had to learn our jitterbug steps. It came off great and the show got some of the highest ratings for The Disney Channel at that time.

For many years, a group of original Mouseketeers (myself, Tommy Cole, Cubby O'Brien, Lonnie Burr, Don Grady, Sharon Baird, Sherry Alberoni, Darlene Gillespie, and Bonni Lynn Fields) performed at Disneyland in special shows at the then Space Stage in Tomorrowland and at the Videopolis Stage near It's a Small World.

In 1980, we celebrated our 25th anniversary with five shows a day featuring 16 numbers performed in each show! I loved doing my specialty jitterbug dance with Sharon. During one of the runs, she was signed by Clint Eastwood to star as Ratboy in a movie of the same name. Darlene filled in and did a great job jitterbugging with me. We even did Sharon's and my big trick, the double wraparound, and the flying Dutchman caught by two Mouseketeer boys after flipping her over my head.

Original Mouseketeers have also appeared at the Disneyana collectors' conventions in Florida at Disney World and occasionally at Disneyland in California. These types of Mouseketeer appearances are ones that we still attend to this day. Luckily, we've been able to work with some great Disney people on these events including Marilyn Magness, our most current Mouseketeer choreographer and global director for Theme Park Entertainment, and Martha Blanding, Merchandising Director at Disneyland, who oversees our get-togethers.

One year, it was just Sherry and I for a show at Walt Disney World in Florida. We were staying at the Contemporary Hotel. Lorraine was with us as well, but she had to take an earlier flight back to Los Angeles and so Sherry and I were left to our own devices (not a good thing since Lorraine orchestrated all our on-site goings-on). We had several hours to kill before we had to head to the airport and Sherry suggested, "Let's go shopping." Since we both love to shop, I thought it was a great idea.

Now just where had we parked our rental car? After wandering around the hotel lot for a while, we finally found it and headed off to the Lake Buena Vista Shopping Center. We were on our way when Sherry turned around and noticed that there was a suitcase in the back seat. She said, "Bobby, you left your bag in the car." I turned around to get a look and said, "It's not my bag, it must be yours." "It's not mine," she replied. Uh oh. We realized we had departed the hotel with someone else's wheels. We had stolen a car!

Did we turn around to return the vehicle? Remember, we only had but a short time to get in our last-minute shopping before leaving Orlando. Decision made—continue to the shopping village, return the "stolen" car later! When we got back to the hotel parking lot we found a couple searching for their rental car. We drove up and apologized, explaining how our key had somehow opened the locks and started their car. Yikes.

One of our most grand promotional trips was to Australia, New Zealand, and Hawaii. It was a three-week whirlwind of meet-and-greets, TV and radio appearances, and newspaper interviews. Sherry and I represented the original Mouseketeers and we were also accompanied by a full-troupe of Disney characters including, of course, Mickey Mouse. Again, Lorraine accompanied us and orchestrated our agendas.

While in Australia, Sherry and I appeared on the *Good Morning America* of that country, *Good Morning Australia*, along with Mickey Mouse. The host was quite a wise guy, and kept repeating that he was going to reveal the person inside the costume and pull off Mickey's head! Having been down that unthinkable path one too many times, Sherry finally shut him down when she said, "Pull off Mickey's head? Mickey's head doesn't come off. Pull off Bobby's head!"

Portraying a Disney character is a very special job. In keeping with the magic of Disney, especially for kids, it's of primary importance that the character is the character, not a person inside a character costume. Of course, the characters have many rules on how they interact with park guests.

One time, when Sherry and I were at Disneyland, we had the extraordinary opportunity to portray a character and really understand what it was like. For a twenty-minute "set", Sherry appeared as Minnie and I became Goofy. We donned our costumes and were sent out into Tomorrowland with a Disney representative.

Then came the kids! I swung one around by the arms in circles as I did with my own children. Wrong! Then I started using my Goofy voice to call out to them, loudly: "Har! Har!" Wrong again! And then an overly eager tot who wanted my attention punched me in the you-know-where. A few teenagers slugged ole Goof and even cussed him out. From that time on, I've had an even greater reverence for those who work so hard literally "becoming" the character they portray and doing so with great finesse. Although I've been called a "character" in the past, this was a different story!

CHAPTER FIFTEEN

All in a Day's Work

Sherry and Lorraine and I had much fun working together over the course of many years. We became somewhat of a traveling Disney promotional trio. One of our escapades involved a Watergate adventure. On this particular trip we were headed to Washington, D.C., from Los Angeles. Because of a very inexperienced limo driver, we were late and missed our plane. Fortunately, our Mouseketeer appearances didn't start until the following day, but we had to wait four hours for the next flight and didn't get into D.C. until midnight, arriving in a fierce thunderstorm.

Lorraine had rented a car and the three of us headed off to our hotel, the famous Watergate. She was driving but had never been to DC before, plus it was late and it was raining. We got very lost, ending up in the wrong part of town. We stopped at a gas station to get directions, but the attendant there wasn't much help. After more driving around, we finally got to the hotel. By now it was about 2am.

Dog tired, we dragged ourselves inside only to find out that because we were so late (we would have been there six hours earlier had we not missed our plane), they had given away our rooms. We begged for accommodations, so they gave Lorraine and Sherry the apartment of someone who was out of town, and I got the Presidential Suite with the proviso that I vacate by 10am because Lady Bird Johnson was coming in. What a view! I could see all the famous American landmarks of our capitol.

Another time, for Mickey's 60th once again, we got limoed, with a police motorcycle escort, down Broadway in New York City where we met then Mayor David Dinkins, and got to throw the switch for a huge Mickey's 60th Disney billboard display in Times Square. The next day, we were escorted to the Circle Line and sailed around Manhattan and to the Statue of Liberty, as guests of former Mayor Koch and *People* magazine. Koch was a big, friendly guy. Afterward, we had lunch with Roy Disney Jr. and his wife.

For Disneyland's 35th Anniversary in 1990, the original emcees from Disneyland's Opening Day TV special—Art Linkletter, Bob Cummings, and former president Ronald Reagan—were on hand to celebrate. They appeared, along with Roy Disney (Walt's nephew), former Disney CEO Michael Eisner, and former Disney COO Frank Wells, on a huge stage constructed in front of the Disneyland train station in Town Square.

Sherry and I were privileged to perform on that stage that day along with two of the new Mouseketeers that were appearing on the Disney Channel show at that time. Before the show, we were escorted backstage where we met Bob, Art, and Ronald Reagan. It was especially a huge honor for me to meet Reagan. He had a twinkle in his eye, and made Sherry and I feel comfortable by telling us a joke.

When the show started, they each went on stage and gave a talk about Disneyland's Opening Day festivities. This was followed by several performances, including one by Sherry and me. At the finale of the show, the entire cast was onstage as confetti cannons shot a barrage of colored paper bits into the air. The blasts sounded very much like gunshots and you could see Reagan quickly duck. After realizing it was just from the confetti being shot out from the Disneyland rooftops, he turned to Michael Eisner with a big smile and said, "Missed me."

When Sherry and I were on another Mickey's 60th excursion to the East coast, it was suggested we help open one of the first Disney stores, in New Jersey. A limo picked us up and we were whisked through the Lincoln Tunnel to our destination. The store was really special, and it was an honor to be there at the beginning of this retail phenomenon.

Sherry and I were very lucky to appear as Disney representatives around the world. Of course, many of the original Mouseketeers were involved in numerous Disney goings-on as well, but we did most of the appearances that required travel, perhaps because the two of us were most available in that we didn't have 9–5 jobs and our families were able to hold down the fort at home. Certainly, we also worked very well together with nary an unkind word between us or with our Mouseketeer chaperone, Lorraine. And we're still doing things together. Not too long ago, Sherry, who is very involved in charitable activities in Orange County, California, "sold" us to a couple at a Catholic charity auction. They paid $5,000 to have lunch with us at Disneyland's exclusive private restaurant, Club 33. Imagine that!

I was sometimes involved in Mouseketeer activites well outside the entertainment sphere. One such occasion involved Mouseketeer Karen Pendleton, Cubby's sidekick during the years of the original show. Sadly, Karen suffered a serious automobile accident in 1983, irreparably injured her spine, and became paralyzed. She has since been confined to a wheelchair. However, she has had a good life, has a wonderful daughter and son-in-law, and is today a doting grandma to several grandkids.

In the latter part of the '80's Karen invited a group of us Mouseketeers to join her in Washington, D.C., for something called Barrier Awareness Day, to bring attention to the plight of handicapped people. Each of Mouseketeer was paired with a disabled person to demonstrate to legislators the obstacles many faced in their everyday lives. I was paired with Karen and so I too used a wheelchair that day, following her around. I became very aware that there were then few wheelchair accessible ramps, and there were times we had to go a block or two out of our way just to get up on the sidewalk from the curb. When I had to use the restroom, I realized that the small stalls were all but impossible to get into. It was all quite eye-opening.

Mouseketeer Lonnie Burr was paired with Geri Jewel, a comedian with cerebral palsy, and he had to lug a weight on his back all day. Another was paired with a blind person, and so on. The experience was one I'll remember forever. It was gratifying to know that we helped shine a bright light on the difficulties handicapped people must deal with every day. Thankfully, many of these obstacles have changed for the better in the ensuing years.

And what are some of my Mouseketeer buddies doing these days?

Sharon Baird, my great dancing partner on *The Mickey Mouse Club*, lives in Reno, Nevada, and has her own business in a ladies hair salon; Darlene Gillespie also resides in Nevada, is retired from having been a surgical nurse, and is a happy grandma; Cubby O'Brien, drummer extraordinaire, lives in the Pacific Northwest with his wife and is semi-retired, although he still occasionally plays music engagements drumming for performers such as Bernadette Peters; Lonnie Burr is an actor and writer also residing in the Pacific Northwest; Doreen Tracey is retired, still lives in southern California, and is involved in numerous new projects; Tommy Cole, whom I often talk with because our sons are best friends, is today an executive of the Make-up Artists union. He and his wife, Aileen, have three handsome grandsons. My pal

Sherry lives in Orange County, California, with her physician husband, Richard Van Meter, and loves being a grandma to her four grandkids.

Having been in the public eye for so many years, my Mouseketeer friends and I have gotten to appear as guests on many well-known TV shows. Sharon and I were on *The Vicki Lawrence Show*, and of course, we were asked to jitterbug. The show was live. At rehearsal, we realized that we'd be dancing on a hard, concrete floor, not the best for dancers. When we were introduced on the live show, we put our all into it and danced full out. But as I flipped Sharon over my shoulder, she landed hard on the cement. She continued dancing, but as soon as we were off air, she could barely put any weight on her foot. Off she went to the Emergency Room. She had sprained her ankle badly, and hobbled out of the hospital on crutches.

On *Dinah's Place*, it was Annette, Cubby, and I appearing together. After the interview, they said we'd be singing "Won't You Play a Simple Melody". So the director says, "Cubby, you play drums, and Bobby, you dance while Annette and Dinah sing." We begin. Now an embarrassing moment: Dinah stops tape and says, "Why is Bobby dancing? Bobby, you're upstaging us, you shouldn't dance." Of course, I related that the director asked me to, but Dinah was not happy. What a great dancing debut with Dinah Shore...that went nowhere.

I was asked to be on *The Rosie O'Donnell Show*, so I thought I'd make her an honorary Mouseketeer. Come to find out, she was expecting Cubby, and on air, she introduces me and under her breath says, "Where's Cubby, where's Cubby. He's my favorite." Guess Cub, who was her first choice, couldn't make it. But the show must go on. I put the ears on her head, sang her the song, and kissed her on her soft cheek.

For all the good times, we've had sadness in our Mouseketeer family, too. Cheryl Holdridge was our first roll-call Mouseketeer to pass away. She succumbed to cancer in June 2009. She was a beautiful blonde little girl who grew up to be a beautiful woman. I was fortunate to speak to her one week before her death when I phoned. At that time, she credited me and our talk at that department store years earlier for inspiring her to get off drugs. She was a well-to-do woman and had no children. She left a good portion of her considerable estate to her closest friend, Mouseketeer Doreen Tracey.

Don Grady, another of our favorite Mouseketeers, passed away in June 2012, also from cancer. Although Don was a Mouseketeer for just one year as a child, he worked with a group of us Mouseketeers when we performed in shows at Disneyland in the '80s and '90s, as well as joining us for special events and meet-and-greet conventions. You probably remember him best as Robbie, one of Fred MacMurray's sons on the long-running hit TV series, *My Three Sons*. In addition to his work as an actor, Don was an accomplished composer and musical arranger.

And of course, we said goodbye to Annette in April 2013. She fought a long and hard battle with multiple sclerosis for over twenty-five years. I remember how saddened we all were when we learned she was suffering from this very debilitating disease. In fact, my wife and I first noticed that there was something wrong when we went to see her and Frankie Avalon perform live at Knott's Berry Farm in an act they ultimately took on the road before Annette was forced to retreat from public life. My astute wife, Kristie, noticed that Annette was a bit unsteady and had to be helped on and off the stage. Kristie and I also noticed that when Annette attended my 50th roller skating birthday party in 1991, our usually fun, participatory Annette wouldn't leave husband Glen's side.

I first heard that Annette had MS when she went public with her illness in 1992. At the time, I was in Cohasset, Massachussetts, performing my Welk act on the road. I sat down and wrote her a note. Just recently I found out that her husband Glen discovered that note. Annette had kept it among her keepsakes. I was amazed. Here is what I wrote on stationary from the Kimball's by the Sea Hotel in Cohasset, Massachussetts. It is dated 7/27/92:

> Dear Annette:
>
> I guess you could call me part of your "Mouse-ka-support" system along with Tommy, Sharon, Lonnie, Sherry, and of course, Lorraine. We're all there for you. I'm on tour at the South Shore Music Circus in Cohasset, Mass., with the Welk Stars, and thought I'd drop you a note.
>
> I realize now why you didn't go skating at my 50th birthday party. But I was so proud you came, and proud to introduce you to everyone.
>
> Did you know I didn't get a traffic ticket recently because of you? Yeah, as I was speeding down Nichols Canyon, a radar cop pulled me over. He recognized me as a Mouseketeer, then said, "I won't give you a ticket if you'll tell me about Annette!" Of course I had to tell him that you were the same as when I first met you thirty-five years ago, down-to-earth, and just the same friendly person you always were.
>
> We have both had the greatest lives so far—our terrific careers but most of all, *our families*.

And I love Lawrence Welk's quote about me, "I never had any trouble with Bobby because he was raised by Walt Disney." We really had a nice foundation professionally at Disney, and also personally.

I like the idea that you're feeling fine, looking great as usual, and have that great husband of yours to help you in any way.

Well, Consentrina, "hope to see you real soon". I'll be thinking of you.

Love, your dancin' mouseka pal, Bobby B.

I'm happy to know that Glen will be auctioning off the handwritten note to raise money for Annette's Research Fund. Lorraine was able to get a copy and sent it to me and it brought it all back.

Throughout her illness, I stayed in touch with Annette. In fact, Kathy Lennon and I would phone her from Branson, Missouri, when we were appearing there at the Welk Champagne Theatre, and try to cheer her up. Kathy had done many Catholic charity benefits with Annette, and they were good friends. At that point, she could not speak, so we carried the conversation the best we could. And although Annette is gone, I know she's probably dancing with Mr. Disney in heaven.

Kristie and me in one of our first photos together.

That wild magazine cover about our engagement.

Our Valentine's Day wedding on February 14th, 1971.

Some of our Mouseketeer attendees at the wedding (L to R): Darlene's husband Phil Gammon, Annette, Annette's husband Jack Gilardi, Darlene Gillespie, Kristie and me, Sharon Baird, Tommy and Aileen Cole, and Doreen Tracey with "Fury's" Bobby Diamond.

I have a dance with my mom. See where I get my enthusiastic smile?!

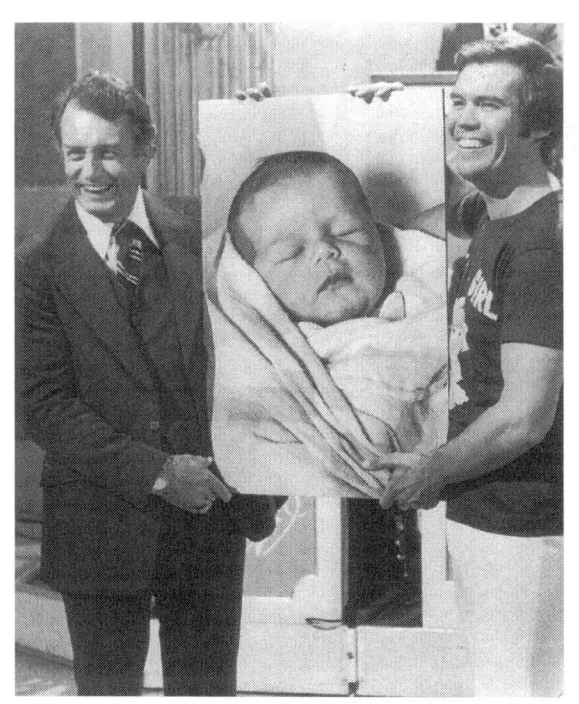

Our first child, Becki Jane, is born, and Lawrence let Myron and me make the announcement on the TV show!

My very favorite picture of my family (L to R): Connor and dad Remon Pagels, Wendi with Charlotte, Robert, Kristie, me, Becki, and Brenton.

The family in Kenya on safari, with Masai people. Our favorite trip.

We were very impressed with Egypt, especially the pyramids and the Sphinx.

Me with four third- and fourth-grade couples at Burgess Cotillion.

Cotillion Master with my four children that teach with me: Brenton, Wendi, Becki, and Robert.

My three grandchildren: Connor, Charlotte, and little Amelia Pagels.

CHAPTER SIXTEEN

Lucky Me

What comment do we hear from younger people today when they approach us about the Welk show? "I was always at Grandma's house on Saturday night, and *The Lawrence Welk Show* was always on. What wonderful memories that show brings back about my growing up," they'd say. "We'd have dinner, and sometimes even polka along with you and your partners."

After all the TV shows, touring, traveling around the world, and having such a full life, what's really most important to me? That's easy—my family, of course. And coming in second, having a wonderful life in my chosen profession. Happiness to me is finding the right spouse and being happy in your work. I got lucky with both.

Kristie and I have been married for over forty years. Now we're "Pappy" and "Granny" to my youngest daughter Wendi's twins, Connor and Charlotte, and their little sister, Amelia. Wendi, 31 years old, is an accredited travel agent, married to her husband Remon who is in the hotel management business. And where did Wendi meet her spouse? On one of our travel adventures when our family took a Caribbean cruise in 1998. Wendi, at age 15, ventured into the Teen Club onboard. At the disco was Remon Pagels, 17. She introduced herself, "Hi, I'm Wendi."

Remon was a Dutchman from The Netherlands, and they just hit it off. They dated cross-continentally for several years and married on May 5, 2002, in a beautiful ceremony at the Sheraton Hotel in Universal City, California. Pastor Bjerke, who had married Kristie and me, and who had christened all four of our kids in the Lutheran church, officiated at Remon and Wendi's wedding.

Remon tried to top me when he proposed to Wendi by popping the question on the back of a camel in the Canary Islands. Even better, I found out later that he was a medalist ballroom dancer in his home country, Holland.

Wendi and Remon set up housekeeping in my boyhood base in Long Beach for several years, along with a stint residing in Las Vegas.

It was during this period that our three grandchildren were born. Our first two, twins Connor and Charlotte, were in-vitro babies, and what a miracle it was to have Wendi deliver such perfect, beautiful twins. She and Remon were living in Las Vegas at the time because he was working at the MGM Grand Hotel there.

Before the babies were born, Wendi invited us to view the ultrasound when the babies were big enough to tell their sex. The doctor located them, took a picture, and labeled it "Big weenie; No weenie." And that's when we knew there was a boy and a girl inside! Kristie, Becki, and I waited in the hospital waiting room on the big day. We were so excited when the happy news was relayed to us. Remon came out to tell us they had a healthy boy and girl. Two little miracles. As many relatives have told us, being Pappy and Granny is the best; spoil 'em and then say bye-bye and return 'em to the folks. As Mouseketeer Sherry once said to us, "Being a grandparent is the only thing in life that's NOT overrated."

After a few years in southern California and Nevada, Wendi had a yen for a European adventure and Remon had a yearning to return to Holland. They pulled up stakes and re-settled in Remon's homeland of the Netherlands. But Wendi had no car, didn't speak the language fluently, missed her family, and after living in sunny southern California, the rainy Dutch climate was a deterrent to both. And besides, NO WALMART! Their planned three- or four-year stay turned into a five-month sojourn. They happily rejoined our close-knit family in the good old USA.

But Kristie and I were not ones to let a travel opportunity pass by. While they were in Holland, the two of us and our two boys visited. We stayed in a nearby camp area called Het Vennenbos where bike riders were everywhere, even paralleling the motorways. We then made side trips to Bruges, Antwerp, and Luxembourg besides seeing more of Holland, including Amsterdam, Delft, Maastricht, and the tiny village of Bladel.

And what are my other three kids doing today? Becki, 37 years old, works in Foley sound effects production at Twentieth Century Fox and is now married to Ian Hardy, who specializes in vintage lighting for Hollywood studios. How she met Ian is an interesting story that involved a very special lamp.

In 1965, I played the Wisconsin State Fair in Janesville. I went shopping in town and bought a wood and fiberglass table lamp.

Growing up, little Becki always loved that lamp, so she took it with her when she moved to her own place to start life on her own.

One day, her cat "The Biter", knocked the lamp down and broke the wooden arm. While the broken lamp sat in a closet, it happened that Becki, Kristie, and I went to a musical in a little theater next to a lamp shop. Becki admired a lamp in the window and I went back the next day and bought it for her for Christmas. "I wonder if that lamp guy in the store could fix my favorite lamp that's broken right now," said Becki.

When she took it in, the shop's Australian owner, Ian, was fixing a lamp behind the counter. He greeted her warmly with his very Australian accent. A few weeks later, Ian called Becki to let her know the lamp was fixed and he'd also put in a new cord. She must have been interested in him because she wore make-up and a nice outfit to the store this time, and Ian asked her out on a date. That's how Becki and her now husband, Ian, met. Ian named the lamp the "Destiny Lamp" and they married on August 19, 2012, the same month and date that Kristie's parents Myron and Berdyne Floren were married. Sharing that anniversary means a lot to Becki. With Remon from The Netherlands and Ian from Australia, I now have two international sons-in-law!

My 35 year-old eldest son, Robert, escorted many guests during his seven-year tenure as a tour guide and three years as a VIP guide for Universal Studios in Hollywood. He's a big fan of the movies, and this job was a very enjoyable one for him, not only to learn more about the studio's history, but also to relay that information to guests. Robert is a graduate of UCLA with a Bachelor of Arts in history. He particularly enjoyed studying ancient Rome and Greece. On a study abroad trip to Italy and Greece, Robert called us one evening to tell us he'd just experienced the best day of his life. He'd visited the Parthenon of the Acropolis in Athens, and that experience touched him very deeply. He is currently a Brand Marketing Coordinator for Universal Studios.

Our youngest son, Brenton, works in the Art Departments at several of the local movie studios. Mostly, he's got Kristie's and my wanderlust. Since he's still a single guy, whenever he can he takes off with his backpack to explore the world on his own, staying in youth hostels, usually finding them just by dropping in. He's 27 years old and makes friends easily, and sometimes hosts them when they crash at his pad on their trips to the U.S. He's been backpacking in Europe, Hawaii, and South America, and will tackle Asia next.

He's had some pretty wild adventures. He dropped his camera in the canals of Venice while taking a photo of a fisherman. Locals came out to help him fish it out with nets and poles, but couldn't reach it. So he risked a 500 euro fine and dove into the canal. He came up with the camera, but also a badly cut finger. A local restaurant owner took him into his restaurant bathroom and sewed up his finger! In the meantime, another local had fetched him some clean dry clothes to put on.

Another favorite adventure was jumping off the 65-foot cliffs of the old city walls of Dubrovnik, Croatia, into the azure sea with the local boys. On the big island of Hawaii, Brent and a hostel friend actually worked on an organic farm for room and board. The farmer was hesitant to hire Brent, being that he was from Hollywood, but at the end of his stint he complimented Brent on his work and asked him to come back any time.

In South America, he made his way to the Inca ruins of Machu Picchu. He's an avid hiker, so while there he hiked up the treacherous mountain of Huayna Picchu across the canyon. In the steamy Amazon, after piranha fishing and feasting, Brent was making his way back to his room down a dark, gas lit path at midnight. He saw a girl coming towards him who had an eerie glow around her. As she got closer, she seemed to hover and had no feet! The next morning he asked about ghosts. The guide asked, "Was it a girl?" A common sighting in the area.

Brent graduated from CSUN (California State University, Northridge), majoring in Media Management. My gift to him? Skydiving, of course!!

As for my beautiful wife, Kristie, she was a stay-at-home mom while the kids grew up, then went back to college to earn a liberal arts degree and a teaching credential. She teaches at a Sylvan Learning Center near our home. She got that fantastic Floren brain, and specializes in math!

Now that we've also taken on the role of grandparents, it's been a blast. Having grandchildren gives me an excuse to relive my Mouseketeer days yet again every time I take them to Disneyland. Our grandkids are also great swimmers, having taken lessons as toddlers (as had our four children), from Greta Andersen, a teacher who was a classic Channel swimmer. It was very important for the kids to take lessons early on, ensuring that summers in our pool are safe and fun backyard adventures. We live near the Los Angeles Zoo, Travel Town with its vintage trains, and Griffith Park with its pony rides and Merry-Go-Round. Each has become a place to take the grandkids. These were the same places Kristie and I took our children, and my folks took me and my siblings when we were growing up. We're now carrying on a three-generation family tradition.

I'm still dancing with Elaine Balden from the Welk show. We appear with Stars of the Lawrence Welk Show in venues around the country. We often work with JoAnn Castle, and Guy and Ralna. We can still cut a mean rug! We recently sold out two days of shows in Chicago with the big band playing behind us. And *The Lawrence Welk Show* is still on television. It's been on for over 60 years. Lawrence must have done something right, especially for someone who only went to school until the fourth grade!

We Welk alumni meet up with each other at monthly luncheons where we talk and laugh about the old days and catch each other up on our current lives. I was so fortunate to have been a part of two family entertainment phenomena of early television, *The Mickey Mouse Club* and *The Lawrence Welk Show*.

As for myself, I continue to make live appearances with a close-knit group of Mouseketeer friends. It's amazing that we were at Disneyland on opening day, July 17, 1955, and we were there to help Michael Eisner open the Disneyland Resort's second theme park, Disney's California Adventure, on February 8, 2001. We've been so much a part of the Disney family, and I'm saving up my energy for the appearances coming up for Disneyland's and *The Mickey Mouse Club's* 60th Anniversary in 2015.

Between *The Mickey Mouse Club* and *The Lawrence Welk Show*, including decades of reruns, I've been on television for nearly sixty years without a break, sometimes up to seven times a week. Not many people can make such a claim.

I'm often asked if people still recognize me. I reply, "Oh yes they do. And if they're ninety, I'm Elvis!"

CHAPTER SEVENTEEN
Farewells

The last time I saw Walt Disney I was headed to Lake Tahoe in 1966 to appear with *The Lawrence Welk Show* at Harrah's Club. I was towing my boat, "The Bubble Machine", behind my Corvette when I noticed a sign that said "Devil's Postpile National Monument". So I veered off to the left, parked, and walked up a hill to see this strange, tall rock formation there in the High Sierras. It was dusk, and not a soul was around.

As I was walking down a path, I glanced up to see an older man walking toward me up the hill with his hat pulled low over his face and head. It was Walt Disney. I said "Walt Disney?" and he replied "Mouseketeer Bobby." I said, "What are you doing here?" He answered, "I bought my daughter a cabin in Mammoth ten years ago, so I wanted to see it. And while I was in the area, I wanted to see Devil's Postpile also." Who would have thought I'd have ever run into Walt Disney in such an unusual place? But I did, and it was the last time I ever saw him. Six months later, he died at age 65 and the world lost one of its most creative geniuses.

Seeing Lawrence Welk for the final time was very sad for me. He was at the Welk office, and he had a touch of dementia. No one was allowed to see him, but Margaret Heron, his secretary of 50 years, slipped me in near the end in 1992.

"Hi, Lawrence, it's me, Bobby! Remember me with Barbara Boylan and my dancing partners Cissy and Elaine?" He nodded with no recognition, said "Hello, young man," and sat at the piano. He had a little parakeet in the office that flew over and landed on his shoulder. He said, "I'd like to play a little song for you." And he played "Over the Waves". He nodded once more, and played it again. Then he said, "I feel tired, nice to see you young man," and left the room to take a nap.

But right before he walked out the door, I said, "Mr. Welk, I loved being on your show, so thank you for giving me some of the most wonderful years of my life." I'll always be grateful to my "musical father" for the opportunity of a lifetime.

As Lawrence Welk always said, "Keep a song in your heart."

I always do.

Acknowledgments

First, I want to thank my mother, Janie Mae Burgess, who not only brought me into this world, but also supported me through all those years driving me to dance lessons and encouraging me to pursue my chosen profession with her upbeat personality. And to dad for his financial support for those lessons.

To my wife, Kristie, my partner in life and love, for typing this book and always being there for me. And to my four children for reminiscing about our fun family times, and listening to my stories.

To my great friend, Lorraine Santoli, thank you for all your time and efforts in editing *Ears and Bubbles*. Your organizational skills putting this book together, and your computer knowledge, amaze me.

Thank you sister Barbara Day, our family "historian", and sister Bette Alward for jogging my memory about those early years.

A special thank you to Walt Disney for giving me my big break with *The Mickey Mouse Club*, and much appreciation to Lawrence Welk for giving me a steady, creative job that I loved all those twenty-one seasons on his television show. And thanks, PBS, for keeping us on the air since 1987.

And last but not least, a great big thank you to all the fans of both of my TV shows for supporting me, and keeping me in the public eye for so many years. It's been a great time.

About the Author

Bobby Burgess got his start in show business on Walt Disney's *Mickey Mouse Club* in 1955, and then starred on *The Lawrence Welk Show* for over two decades, marrying bandleader Myron Floren's daughter. Today, he operates the Burgess Cotillion, where children can learn ballroom dance, manners, and etiquette. He still appears at events nationwide for The Disney Company and *The Lawrence Welk Show*.

To learn more about the Burgess Cotillion, visit: http://bobbyburgesscotillion.com

About the Publisher

Theme Park Press is the largest independent publisher of Disney and Disney-related pop culture books in the world.

Established in November 2012 by Bob McLain, Theme Park Press has released best-selling print and digital books about such topics as Disney films and animation, the Disney theme parks, Disney historical and cultural studies, park touring guides, autobiographies, fiction, and more.

For more information, and a list of forthcoming titles, please visit:

ThemeParkPress.com

More Books from Theme Park Press

To see all our books, visit ThemeParkPress.com

Made in the USA
Middletown, DE
15 January 2020